A LITTLE HISTORY OF THE
ENGLISH COUNTRY CHURCH

Sir Roy Strong was educated at the University of London and the Warburg Institute. He joined the staff of the National Portrait Gallery in 1959 and became its director from 1967 to 1973. He was director of the Victoria & Albert Museum from 1974 to 1987, when he resigned to become a full-time writer, broadcaster and consultant. He is also High Bailiff and Searcher of the Sanctuary at Westminster Abbey and an altar server at Hereford Cathedral. His books include *The Story of Britain*, *The Arts in Britain*, *Feast: A History of Grand Eating* and, most recently, *Coronation*.

ALSO BY ROY STRONG

The Renaissance Garden in England

A Country Life

The Story of Britain

The Spirit of Britain

Feast: A History of Grand Eating

Gloriana

The Arts in Britain

The Laskett

Painting the Past

Passions Past And Present

Coronation: A History of Kingship and the
British Monarchy

ROY STRONG

A Little History of the English Country Church

VINTAGE BOOKS
London

Published by Vintage 2008

2 4 6 8 10 9 7 5 3 1

First published in Great Britain in 2007 by
Jonathan Cape
Random House, 20 Vauxhall Bridge Road,
London SW1V 2SA

www.vintage-books.co.uk

Addresses for companies within The Random House Group
Limited can be found at: www.randomhouse.co.uk/offices.htm

The Random House Group Limited Reg. No. 954009

A CIP catalogue record for this book
is available from the British Library

ISBN 9781844138302

The Random House Group Limited supports The Forest
Stewardship Council (FSC), the leading international forest
certification organisation. All our titles that are printed on
Greenpeace approved FSC certified paper carry the FSC logo.
Our paper procurement policy can be found at
www.rbooks.co.uk/environment

Mixed Sources
Product group from well-managed
forests and other controlled sources
www.fsc.org Cert no. TT-COC-2139
© 1996 Forest Stewardship Council
FSC

Typeset by Palimpsest Book Production Limited,
Grangemouth, Stirlingshire

Printed and bound in Great Britain by
CPI Cox & Wyman, Reading RG1 8EX

To A. N. Wilson

CONTENTS

Preface   1

Introduction   5

1   In the Beginning   11

2   People's Theatre   29

3   Obedience   61

4   Silence and Ambiguity   85

5   The Beauty of Holiness   121

6   Collapse and Fragmentation   143

7   The Parting of the Ways   165

8   The Rainbow Comes and Goes   197

Epilogue   225

Bibliography   237

List of Illustrations   247

Index   255

Preface

IN 1977 THE VICTORIA AND Albert Museum staged an exhibition entitled *Change and Decay: The Future of Our Churches*. It was the second in a series of exhibitions on the plight of the historic environment, staged during my directorship of the museum in the 1970s; the two others covered the country house (1974) and the garden (1979). The latter are still regarded as landmarks changing both the public and the government's perception by creating a shocked awareness of the enormity of the losses that were threatening our architectural and horticultural heritage. Consequently their causes do no longer need to be pleaded. Indeed, the country house has become a popular attraction, and every kind of historic garden – from great palace gardens to municipal parks – has been restored over the last decades.

The exhibition on the future of our churches had to compete with an exhibition on Fabergé, and as a rather doom-laden topic it seemed ill-chosen for the Queen's Silver Jubilee. Yet although it attracted only about 20,000 visitors – many a time I strolled through the exhibition alone, for it was empty – within three weeks of opening, the government, for the first time, pledged money for restoration projects. But in the long run churches never gained the support enjoyed by country houses and gardens, and as a result, the future of the thousands of country churches remained uncertain. After thirty years, I have now returned to the subject out of a sense of urgency: I strongly believe that we have reached a crisis point that calls for immediate action if we want to save our country churches. If, in terms of our heritage, the twentieth century was about saving the country house, the twenty-first will be about saving our great historic churches.

It was my friend A. N. Wilson who first put into my head the idea that I should write a book of this kind for an audience who had forgotten, or perhaps never known, what had taken place in parish churches over the centuries. In 1977 I wrote in the Preface to the *Change and Decay* exhibition catalogue:

> Seldom are we ever given a glimpse of the [church] building as the historic microcosm over the centuries of a community. Their very fabric tells us of prosperity and depression, of war and peace; extensions in size reflect rise in population; the names of the headstones reveal the families who for generations moulded the life pattern of the land around. We need to develop for a wider public our approach to churches as expressions of past human beings, everyone's ancestors over the centuries, and shift from the crudity of categorising a building on its aesthetic merits alone, ignoring all else.

This remains as true today as it was thirty years ago. Hence this little book.

This introductory history could never have been written without drawing on the pioneering work of distinguished academics, who during the last few decades have rewritten the religious history of England and revolutionised our understanding of such tumultuous events as the Reformation. I must single out Eamon Duffy's *The Stripping of the Altars* as the greatest inspiration: a book of that breadth and historical imagination is needed for every period in history.

Telling the story of religious life in England from Anglo-Saxon times is a vast topic and one could labour on it for years. In writing it I have inevitably had to simplify a complex story. This is not the place to sketch greater historical developments or explain theological concepts, and although the visual beauty of the country church lies at the heart of this little book, it is not an architectural history or a guide to church interiors and symbolism. Those readers wanting to explore further the many themes which my book can only touch on are referred to the Bibliography, where I have marked those titles I can recommend as 'Further Reading'. I should add that after the Reformation I had to confine my canvas to Anglican churches, although I am of course aware of many similar problems facing Roman Catholic churches and those of the various Protestant denominations today.

We urgently need a book that addresses the impending crisis of the English country church and that explains to a large audience what will be lost for ever if we fail to act now. This book tells the story of what ordinary people experienced when they attended church on Sunday. It is a people's history: I have tried to describe how their lives found expression in that unique place of worship and how they were affected by the dramatic changes that took place within it over the centuries.

In writing this, friends have responded to this or that query and helped me on my way, among them the Very Reverend Michael Tavinor, the Reverend Christopher Kevill-Davies, Pamela Tudor-Craig (Lady Wedgwood) and Dr Richard Barber. Juliet Brightmore has once again successfully gathered in the pictures. I am especially grateful to the Reverend Nicholas Sagovsky, Canon Theologian at Westminster Abbey, who read the entire text in the interests of theological accuracy, and, last but by no means least, to my editor, Jörg Hensgen, without whom there would have been no book.

Roy Strong
The Laskett
March 2007

Introduction

EVERY VILLAGE HAS A CHURCH. Scattered around England are some 16,000 parish churches, and the vast majority of them can be found in the countryside. They come in every size and occupy every kind of site. Some loom like minor cathedrals, others nestle like large dog kennels, hardly arising above the headstones that punctuate the surrounding churchyard. Some are sited at the heart of the village, others on its fringes. Some perch on hillsides, others arise out of a valley. They can be built in stone, brick or wood. They equally manifest themselves in every architectural style – Norman, Gothic, Classical, Victorian revival, and Arts and Crafts.

English country churches continue to have an extraordinary hold over a nation now often defined as 'post-Christian'. People seem instinctively attracted to the crumbling stone and lichen, to the overgrown churchyards and to the topsy-turvy of ancient headstones. Thousands of visitors are irresistibly drawn to walk up the churchyard path and throw open the door. No one has caught this mood so well as the poet Philip Larkin:

> Once I am sure there's nothing going on
> I step inside, letting the door thud shut.
> Another church: matting, seats and stone,
> And little books; sprawlings of flowers, cut
> For Sunday, brownish now; some brass and stuff
> Up at the holy end; the small neat organ;
> And a tense, musty, unignorable silence
> Brewed God knows how long. Hatless, I take off
> My cycle-clips in awkward reverence.

It is easy to forget that country-church visiting of this kind is a relatively new phenomenon, born of the age of the car. But the fact that so many want to visit them we owe to a large degree to two great cultural voices – Nikolaus Pevsner and John Betjeman.

Pevsner was a German exile, Jewish by birth but a Lutheran convert. He came to England in 1935, bringing with him a rigour of art historical scholarship previously absent in this country. His most celebrated and still indispensable work is *The Buildings of England*, published in forty-six volumes between 1951 and 1974. The fact that this monumental work is still in print over thirty years on speaks for itself. The entries on churches work to a set formula: the architecture of each church is described and then follows a list of furnishings, monuments, benches, stained glass and so on. In short, we are presented with an inventory of its contents; listing the plate is as near as Pevsner gets to indicating the use of the building. But what is missing – and perhaps bearing in mind the sheer scale of his project understandably so – is any response to the atmosphere of the place or any broader information that would explain the social and spiritual context of the building. Pevsner recorded churches like a scientist dissecting a specimen. These are unpeopled buildings; yet churches after all are as much about people as they are about God.

While Pevsner speaks to the intellect, John Betjeman speaks to the heart and the imagination. Poet, writer and broadcaster, Betjeman was a revered national treasure of the second half of the twentieth century. He opposed modernism – which Pevsner championed – and one senses that Betjeman objected to this German academic pontificating on things that are essentially English. Betjeman's writing was accessible and attracted a vast audience that knew him through radio and television. Betjeman, far more than Pevsner, was to frame how Everyman was to look at the country church in the late twentieth century. It is a viewpoint which is overwhelmingly nostalgic and patriotic, one born of a country at war. The tone was set in the opening paragraph of a series of radio talks he gave in 1948:

> Down what lanes, across how many farmyards, nesting in
> how many valleys, topping what hills and suddenly appearing
> round the corners of what ancient city streets are the
> churches of England? The many pinnacles in Somerset, of
> rough granite from the moors in Devon and Cornwall, of
> slate by the sea coasts, brushed with lichen, spotted with
> saffron, their rings of five and six bells pouring music among
> the windy elm trees as they have poured their sound for
> centuries, still they stand, the towers and spires of the West.

The rhythm of the language suffuses them with a poetic aureole. *The Collins Guide to English Parish Churches*, which Betjeman edited and which appeared in 1958, was concerned with 'judging the buildings by their atmosphere and aesthetic merit'. It listed not only medieval and early modern churches but also embraced those built in the Victorian age and the early twentieth century, which had been ignored previously.

In his introductions to particular counties Betjeman was delightfully opinionated. The fact that he was a committed Anglican of Catholic leaning shines through the book, and its atmosphere breathes the aesthetic patriotism of his great friend, the painter John Piper. While Pevsner never mentioned what a church was used for, Betjeman was unequivocal in the last sentence of his general introduction: '. . . the purpose of the church remains the same . . . to be a place where the Faith is taught and the Sacraments are administered'.

There has been no lack of books about churches in recent years but the only one to challenge these two founts has been Simon Jenkins's *England's Thousand Best Churches*, published in 1999. A prolific journalist and columnist by profession, Jenkins takes a very different line from both Pevsner and Betjeman, casting churches in a manner acceptable to the prevailing secularism at the turn of the millennium. He states categorically that to him 'a church is not a place of revealed truth', but, in the words of the poet Thomas Gray, of 'the short and simple annals of the poor'. But although in part the latter may be true, the former most certainly is not. For those who built them and those who worshipped – and, like myself, still worship – in them, they *are* places of revealed truth. Although I would certainly agree with him that a church is 'a dispersed gallery of vernacular art', I would dispute his conclusion, 'A church is a museum': as long as one Christian remains to say a prayer within its walls a church is not a museum.

A church and its surrounding land is sacred space, blessed and set aside to God. The reader who visits these buildings today may not believe in God, but should respect those who once did and still do. I am constantly struck by how people instinctively respect a church on entering it, doffing their hats and lowering their voices. They do not *behave* as they would in a museum. Artefacts there have been removed from the context of faith and become exhibits in the history of art, but the things left in the country church retain their framework of religious function and collective memory.

And all of this brings me to why I have written this little book. When Betjeman and Pevsner were writing in the 1950s what went on in a church was a given. Most people had been brought up as church-goers, even if now lapsed, and were familiar with the liturgy. All that can no longer be taken for granted, as I am constantly reminded at events such as Thanksgivings when, if the Lord's Prayer has not been printed in the service sheet, there is a mumbled embarrassment. Here is an attempt to tell those who love visiting these beautiful buildings what went on inside them and in some form, however truncated, still does today. This little history is written for all those who, like Philip Larkin, cannot resist pushing open that door.

Chapter 1

In the Beginning

THE CHURCH OF ST MARY and St David at Kilpeck lies only a few miles from where I live on the Welsh Borders in south Herefordshire. Virtually anyone who comes to stay is taken to see this most perfect of churches, constructed from the local red sandstone in the mid-twelfth century. Few churches more vividly demonstrate that even five centuries after the arrival of St Augustine's mission of 597 there still lurked beneath the Christian surface a strong pagan veneer. On the outside, the corbels around the chancel end portray grotesque animals, including a rabbit and a dog, alongside the Christian *Agnus Dei*, the Lamb of God, and the visitor is confronted with an obscene depiction of the Earth Mother, her two hands extending her genitals to large proportions. The interior too shows a figure from the pagan past, for at the centre of the vault, immediately over the altar, the face of a green, or tree, man looks down on the visitor, fronds of greenery sprouting from and around his face.

This church was originally part of a large complex that included a castle – the mount of which is still visible from the west end of the church – and a Benedictine priory founded in 1134. The style of the architecture is what we call Norman or Romanesque – heavy and definite, more challenging than welcoming. But at Kilpeck that minatory quality is softened by sculptural decoration of exceptional beauty. Inside the church, the chancel arch has shafts bearing haloed saints, one arising upwards from another; outside, the south door is embraced by an arch showing the signs of the zodiac and a tympanum that depicts the Tree of Life. On either side the supporting shafts sport writhing dragons and warrior figures whose stylistic origins lie in Scandinavia – a legacy from Viking times before the Norman Conquest.

Today the country church belongs to a configuration of buildings which we have come to regard as immemorial – the timeless

The pagan underlay at St Mary and
St David, Kilpeck: the Earth Mother corbel.

tableau of England formed by the great house, the church and the
village. But the mix of pagan and Christian symbolism at Kilpeck helps
us to understand that the country church was once a novelty: here we
can see this English tableau in the making.

Christianity was an urban religion brought to England by traders from
the ports of the Eastern Mediterranean in the second century AD. It
had been the faith of a persecuted minority until the Emperor
Constantine granted the Christians freedom of worship in 313; from
the late fourth century Christianity became the state religion of the
Roman Empire. During the time of persecution it had been impossible
to create permanent places of worship. But this disinterest in buildings fully accorded with the views of the writers of the New Testament
for whom the church was not a visible structure but the Body of Christ
and the Temple of the Holy Spirit: Christians formed the Church wherever they gathered together. In Roman Britain they would have congre-
gated in a room in a villa, which might have been decorated with
motifs that the initiated would have recognised as Christian. On the

The chancel at Kilpeck.

mosaic floor of the fourth-century villa at Hinton St Mary in Dorset, for instance, we find the image of Christ against the background of the sacred monogram, the chi-rho.

The so-called Dark Ages, which followed the withdrawal of the Romans, have left us no evidence of what happened to Christian life, and the story only begins to pick up with the re-Christianisation of England by Celtic missionaries from Ireland. First, wooden and, later, stone crosses were erected to mark the places where they preached and administered the sacraments. A considerable number of the stone crosses have survived, many of them intact. We can only speculate about the early history of church building but the progression from an open-air assembly to, first, some kind of temporary, and then permanent, covering for both priest and congregation seemed inevitable.

In 597, St Augustine and his monks arrived from Rome 'with all things necessary for the worship of the church, namely sacred vessels, altar linen, ornaments, priestly vestments, and relics of holy apostles and

Celtic cross at Lindisfarne on Holy Island, Northumberland.

martyrs'. While the Celtic Church had been both monastic and tribal – where missionaries fanned out from monasteries to preach the word wherever they chose to erect their crosses – Augustine brought to the British Isles a church-centred Christianity. Pope Gregory the Great had instructed the missionaries to take over the pagan temples, to destroy the idols and then to have 'holy water sprinkled into the temples, altars built, and relics set there. So the people will have no need to change their places of concourse. And where of old they were wont to sacrifice oxen to demons, in this matter also there should be some substitution of solemnity . . .' Thus Christianity subsumed elements of the old pagan beliefs and some of our oldest parish churches replaced pagan temples.

In this way England was evangelised, from the north and west by missionaries from Ireland, and from the south-east by those from Rome. Both Churches had their own liturgical traditions and there were significant differences, such as the date of Easter, but all this was settled in favour of the Roman rite at the Synod of Whitby in 664. Yet we know little of what happened on the ground in these rural areas. We can assume that small portable altars were set up, but how Mass was said exactly it is impossible to tell. As the Mass and its successor, Holy Communion or the Lord's Supper, are so central to our story, we need to understand at the outset the origins and evolution of this rite.

Early Christian worship had centred on a shared communal meal, the *agape*, which would be followed by the Eucharist (from the Greek word for thanksgiving), the symbolic re-enactment of the Last Supper in which those present partook of the bread and wine as the Body and Blood of Christ. This act is grounded in the teaching of the New Testament. During the first centuries of the Church various forms of worship developed that centred on the consecration of bread and wine followed by their distribution to the congregation. Greek had been the language of the early Christians (it still is in the East) but with the dominance of Rome that was gradually overtaken by Latin. By the close of the fourth century two main rites for the Mass in the West had emerged – the Roman and the Gallican. The Roman rite was originally relatively simple and austere, while the Gallican rite was more sensuous, symbolical and dramatic, celebrated with splendid ceremonial and an abundance of incense and prayers. However, by the later Middle Ages the Roman rite had accrued a sense of spectacle with the introduction of the Elevation of the Host – the holding aloft of the consecrated bread, by then in wafer form, for adoration – the use of incense and lights and bell-ringing. What little we know of the rite of the Celtic Church stemmed from the Gallican, albeit with local variations, but in the aftermath of the Synod of Whitby in 664 it was the Roman rite which prevailed in England.

In 668 Pope Vitalian sent to England a Greek monk, Theodore of Tarsus, and instructed him to reconcile the conflicting Christian parties in the aftermath of the Synod. In the case of the liturgy Theodore made concessions, accepting Celtic liturgical practices and integrating them into the Roman rite. From the Celtic tradition also came many of the dramatic and symbolic ceremonies that punctuated the liturgical year, such as the blessing of candles at Candlemas, commemorating the Purification of the Virgin and the presentation of Christ in the Temple; the imposition of ashes on Ash Wednesday, marking the beginning of the penitential season of Lent; the blessing of palms on Palm Sunday in remembrance of Jesus' entry into Jerusalem prior to his crucifixion; and many of the Holy Week ceremonies, to which I will return in the next chapter. The result was in effect a mixed rite to which was added, during the eleventh century, the recitation of the Creed and the offertory, or the bidding prayers, which were said in the vernacular. Later still was added the opening of the Mass as we know it today: the recitation by the priest of Psalm 43, 'Judica me', the Confiteor, or confession, and other preparatory prayers by the priest said at the foot of the altar.

What eventually prevailed in the English country church became known as the Sarum rite. By tradition compiled by Osmund, bishop of Salisbury, at the close of the eleventh century for use in the cathedral church, it brought together all these different elements and became the standard throughout most of England. Its sense of drama and splendour differed greatly from the simpler Roman rite and was to penetrate even the humblest of parish churches.

The basic structure of our present parish system developed in the tenth century. The Anglo-Saxon ecclesiastical system centred on the minster, or *monasterium*; these were major churches with attendant buildings that housed priests servicing the outlying areas. The minsters had emerged after the conversion to Christianity of the separate kingdoms in England, when the kings founded central

An unaltered Anglo-Saxon church: St Laurence, Bradford-on-Avon, Wiltshire, eighth to eleventh century.

churches that accommodated communities of monks, nuns or priests. This system survived both the Viking invasions and the Norman Conquest in 1066.

The next stage in the development of the parish system was the building of small churches by local lords for their families, tenants and serfs, resulting in the so-called 'Great Rebuilding' from 1050 to 1150 (although it has been argued that many of these churches probably date from much earlier times). The minsters went into eclipse as local churches multiplied in response to the emergence of both self-contained manors presided over by thegns and by the village as a new rural social unit. Such a configuration demanded a new ecclesiastical system to service it. Thus the origins of the parish church lie in these twin pressures: the demand from below for a local church serving the local community, and equally from on high by a lord for a church that he could control. In 1050 Bishop Herman of Ramsbury reported to Pope Leo IX about 'England being filled everywhere with churches, which daily were being added anew in new places; about the distribution of innumerable ornaments and bells in oratories; about the most ample liberality of kings and rich men for the inheritance of Christ.'

That shift to local places of worship was reflected in other developments. Increasingly the ruling classes were no longer buried in the minster but within the confines of the nascent parish church. More important, however, was the emergence of religious guilds, which also marked a move away from the monastic monopoly of religion. The guilds were composed of lay people and were concerned at this time in the main with burial rites and memorial Masses for their members. But in practice it meant that for the first time there was a group of lay people active in the service of the church, whose responsibilities would later, during the twelfth and thirteenth centuries, extend to the maintenance of the church fabric, the support of the clergy and the administration of alms to the poor.

Thus by 1150 the majority of medieval parish churches were in existence, and by 1200 the parochial system had crystallised. Each diocese was headed by a bishop and consisted of a set of parishes. The size of the district was variable, for neither the ecclesiastical nor the lay author-ities had any control over the building of churches; the overwhelming majority of parish churches were built by laymen who regarded the building as their personal property. Where a village had more than one lord, there could be two churches or a 'shared ownership' that included the right to present the cleric. This lack of any overall planning resulted in a very uneven provision of parish churches. Their distribution reflected ancient landownership, and even today it is sometimes possible to trace the outline of a tenth-century Anglo-Saxon estate by following the parish boundary. It was not until the middle of the thirteenth century that the Church in England became an organised body containing some 9,500 parishes under the increasing control of the bishops.

The English word 'church' derives from the Greek, meaning 'thing belonging to the Lord'. In Old English it was spelled *cirice* and *circe*, and in Middle English, the vernacular of the Middle Ages, that trans-muted into *chereche, chiriche, chirche* and, finally, *churche*. As the church belonged to God it was sacrosanct, and in times of trouble it was into the church and the surrounding churchyard that villagers took their chattels and drove their stock – the encircling walls and hedges trans-formed into a stockade.

At the same time, we witness the emergence of the church as a recog-nisable building. Augustine had brought with him a monk familiar with the churches of the Byzantine Empire, and consequently the earliest churches in England were adaptations from the classic basilica design of early Christian architecture. The basilica consisted of a rectangular nave, which accommodated the congregation, and a semi-circular apse, or chancel, for the altar. In Kent these churches originally had a triple arch screening the chancel in homage to the Trinity, which then gave way to a single arch. Another feature were the *porticus*, a plural word

Anglo-Saxon tower and chancel at St Peter, Barton upon Humber, Humberside, tenth century.

meaning 'little porches', which were small chambers off the nave, chancel and, later, under the tower which could house vestries or tombs. In Northumbria churches adopted the Celtic tradition of erecting high stone crosses outside and within had narrow naves and small square chancels with a single arch. After 1000, towers became widespread, one of which survives at Barton upon Humber on Humberside.

By that time, a new building style had arrived from the continent. There the Carolingian Empire under Charlemagne in the ninth century had triggered a Christian revival and an architectural style we call Romanesque, which owed its inspiration to the earliest Christian basilicas, and it was in this style that the many churches arising during the Great Rebuilding were constructed. Churches now became larger and the apse gradually disappeared in favour of a rectangular chancel with a large east window. The *porticus* too vanished, evolving into the transept that gives us the familiar cruciform plan of virtually every country church. In addition, after 1130 we witness an astonishing proliferation of decorative sculpture, which is so clearly evident at Kilpeck and which we describe today as the age of the zigzag.

As the congregations grew side aisles were created. The first of these would have been to the north where it caused the least disruption; few wished to be buried on the dark side of the cemetery, and expansion to the south would also have necessitated the demolition of the porch. In order to restore light to the nave after the addition of an aisle, an arcade of pillars was introduced, which supported a clerestory filled with windows. As congregations continued to grow, a south aisle would eventually be added. In this most basic form lie the architectural origins of virtually every country church; what follows is simply elaboration.

We know little about what actually happened in church during this early period. It has been suggested that the chancel arch may have been curtained to hide the sacred mysteries during Mass. The great prominence given to the porch in Romanesque churches – elaborately decorated with the tympanum figures of the enthroned Christ or St Michael slaying the dragon – indicate its importance: the porch was the gateway to the Christian life. Moreover, we know from the later Middle Ages how important the porch was: it was here that business was transacted, oaths sworn, bargains struck, disputes settled, marriages solemnised and part of the baptismal rite conducted. Inside the church, the dominant feature would have been the Rood above the chancel arch, depicting Christ on the cross flanked by the Virgin and his beloved disciple John. As they were almost always made of wood, hardly any Roods have survived the iconoclasm of the Reformation; all that remains of the Rood at St Laurence, Bradford-upon-Avon, are two battered flying angels.

Evidence that Roods were the norm points to a central feature of all medieval church interiors: the omnipresence of images. Pope Gregory the Great, who sent Augustine to England in 597, laid down the principal reasons for their use: 'For a picture is introduced into a church so that those who are ignorant of letters may at least read by looking at the walls what they cannot read in books.' This emphasis led to increasing elaboration in the internal decoration of parish churches. Pope Gregory's justification of images was echoed time and again throughout the Middle Ages. John Mirk, prior of the canons regular of Lilleshall in Shropshire, wrote around 1400: 'I say boldly that there are many thousands of people that could not imagine in their hearts how Christ was crucified if they did not learn it by looking at sculpture and painting.'

In order to comprehend the importance of images we need to understand the medieval mindset. Today we take reading, writing and visual stimulation for granted. We encounter more images in a day than a medieval villager would have seen in a lifetime. Yet virtually the only images he or she ever saw were displayed in the parish church: the statue of the Virgin over the porch, the interior depicting stories from the Bible, the Last Judgement or Doom, and images of the Virgin and the saints. There would also be the sculpted figures of the Rood and those of saints attached to various altars. As stained glass became more common from the twelfth century, the windows too were a phantasmagoria of images. The impact of this visual world on the many worshippers who were unable to read or write must have been overwhelming: spelled out before their eyes was the whole story of Creation and Salvation – and their own place within it.

St Augustine had also brought with him to England relics of the apostles and martyrs. From the earliest times of the Church, the bodies of those who had suffered for the Christian faith had been venerated. In Rome churches such as St Peter's were built over the tombs of saints, and the Second Council of Nicaea laid down in 787 that no church should be consecrated without them. Relics made tangible the story of the Gospel and the lives of the saints. As time passed the churches in this country would display the relics of English saints and martyrs, and the earliest reliquary caskets that survive – like the Roods, many were destroyed at the Reformation – date from the late twelfth

Enamelled chalice, *c.* 1200.   Paten, thirteenth century.

century and contain the relics of St Thomas Becket, who was martyred in 1170. Important relics were a major attraction of the greater abbeys and cathedrals such as Durham and Canterbury, which soon became the main pilgrimage centres.

Over this whole domain presided the clergy. Up until the twelfth century priests could be married; thereafter clerical celibacy was enforced, although concubinage continued to be common. The right of presentation to a benefice pertained to a lord, bishop or monastery, who would take the major part of the church's endowment, including the tithe, a tenth of the congregation's crops and livestock. This left the priest with only a fraction of the church's income, together with what was given at the offertory on great feast days, such as Easter and Christmas, and the land with which the church was endowed, known as the glebe. John of Ford's life of St Wulfric gives us a unique insight into the life of a priest in the 1130s. Wulfric was a hermit at Haselbury in Somerset, where the priest was one Brictric. Married with one son, Brictric was a poor man extracting a living from the soil, which he worked with his own hands, and his income was only supplemented by the tithe. When he was not working the land, he spent day and night in the parish church chanting psalms and praying, fulfilling the prime duty of a medieval priest: the perpetual adoration of God.

The clergy's material condition did not improve until the Lateran Council of 1215, which laid down that the priest had the right of freehold of his benefice, in which case the cleric became a vicar. If he was one of the monks from the monastery that had the right of presentation and appropriated all the revenues, the priest was called rector. It was a sad fact that churches in the early Middle Ages were viewed as sources of enrichment. As fees were even exacted for the sacrament of marriage by both landlord and church, until the thirteenth century most peasant couples set up home together without the benefit of matrimony.

The Lateran Council also formally enunciated the doctrine of transubstantiation, which defined how by a change in their 'substance' the bread and wine at Mass became the very Body and Blood of Christ. The reservation of the Host in a pyx suspended above the high altar now became mandatory and it was stipulated that everyone should receive the Sacrament at least once every year. At the same time, responsibility for the upkeep of the chancel was given to whoever had the right of presentation, while the nave along with the ornaments, vestments and the churchyard pertained to the laity. This put a heavy burden on the congregation and led to the emergence of vestries, gatherings of the laity to raise funds, and churchwardens, whose task it was to administer them.

The chancel now became the focal point of the church. It was stipulated that there had to be a large stone altar with five consecration crosses representing the five wounds of Christ. The chancel was now also divided from the nave by a wooden pierced screen; one of the earliest of these, dating from the mid-thirteenth century, can be seen at Stanton Harcourt in Oxfordshire. Close to the altar stood a piscina for the ablutions, a feature that can be traced back to the ninth century. The seating of the clergy was arranged in the form of the sedilia, a row of three stone seats set into the south wall in ascending

Font, St Michael, Castle Frome, Herefordshire, twelfth century.

order for the priest, deacon and subdeacon during Mass. In the north wall there was the aumbry, a cupboard that housed the sacred vessels: the paten for the Host and the chalice for the wine. A wooden lectern, often in the form of an eagle, symbol of St John the Evangelist, was also placed in the chancel. Yet while a long list of ornaments and vestments was also required, records of episcopal visitations reveal that many churches lacked even the most basic liturgical vessels and service books, and few had any vestments at all. The situation gradually improved as the Middle Ages progressed, but these requirements put a heavy financial burden on the congregation.

In the main body of the church stood the font, originally a tub for total immersion but later becoming a circular or polygonal container in which the sanctified water was kept under lock and key. Baptism was now practised by affusion whereby water was poured over the head of the candidate as part of an elaborate symbolic rite, which also included anointing with holy oil. The floor of the nave was earthen and there were no seats or benches, so the faithful stood or knelt on the ground, sometimes men at the front and women at the back, sometimes women and men on either side of the aisle. There was no heating or lighting: candles on the altar only appeared at the close of the twelfth century. Churchgoing remained a rigorous experience for several generations.

Yet the church had become a mysterious place midway between Heaven and Earth. The rites that were performed here had a powerful, mystical aura, for they were conducted in Latin, a language incomprehensible to most even when it later became mandatory to learn the Paternoster, the Ave Maria and the Creed by rote. And the interplay between Heaven and Earth was re-enacted every Sunday when the village gathered in church to witness the miracle of the Mass.

Chapter 2

People's Theatre

WHEN I FIRST VISITED THE church of Long Melford in Suffolk in 1962, it left an indelible impression on account of its size and splendour. Long Melford is an ordinary parish church; few churches, however, are over 250 feet long. If evidence were needed that the late medieval Church was a vigorous institution, one need not look further than this noble monument to the last phase of the Gothic style, the perpendicular, which turned churches into lanterns of light. Long Melford was rebuilt at the close of the fifteenth century by two rich families, but everywhere we look we find evidence that this great church was a project that embraced the whole community. Inscriptions in the south side-windows reveal the contributions made by individual members of the congregation: 'Pray for the sowl of Rog: Muriell of whose goods this arch was made'; or 'Pray for the sowl of John Pie and Aly his wife, of whos good this arch was made and thes twey wydowy glasid.'

Today the church is a shell, stripped bare by the iconoclasm of the Reformation, then overlaid again with the visual trappings of Catholic worship in the late Victorian period. At Long Melford, however, we have something utterly unique: a record of what the church had looked like before the great cataclysm of the Reformation. During the reign of Elizabeth I, Roger Martyn, a member of one of the two families who had paid for the majority of the rebuilding, was a recusant who had withdrawn from attending the parish church. He left an account of the world that had been destroyed. Over the High Altar, he writes, there had been a triptych of gilded wood 'carved very artificially with the Story of Christ's Passion ... lively and beautifully set forth'. It was 'made of one great Tree' and would have been one of those wood carvings depicting scenes of the Passion filled with a multitude of participants that can still be seen today in German churches. The triptych had

Holy Trinity, Long Melford, Suffolk.

'very fair boards, made to shut too, which were opened upon high and solemn feast dayes, which then was a very beautiful shew'. On either side of the altar were tabernacles, which reached to the roof of the chancel. The one to the north showed an image of the Trinity, to which the church was dedicated; that to the south is likely to have contained a statue of the Virgin. The chancel was divided from the nave by a feature that became universal in late medieval churches: a decorated wooden rood-screen. Martyn recorded that the one at Long Melford contained, along its lower half, a frieze depicting the Apostles. Above, there was the Rood itself, showing Christ on the cross flanked by Mary and John, and a gallery with 'a fair pair of organs', indicating that the services were accompanied by music and choral singing. Roger Martyn recalled how each Good Friday it was from this gallery that a priest sang the story of the Passion. He also remembered the Easter Sepulchre, which was erected during Holy Week in the chancel to receive the conse- crated Host: 'a fair painted frame of timber ... with holes for a number of fair tapers to stand in before the Sepulchre, and to be lighted in service time'.

In 'my Ile called "Jesus Ile"' was his own family chapel. Martyn described a picture of the Crucifixion over the altar, which was flanked on one side by Christ 'holding a round bowle in his hand signifying I think that he containeth the whole round world', and on the other by the image of 'Our Lady of Pity', the Virgin 'having the afflicted body of her dear Son, as he was taken down off the Cross lying on her lap, the tears as it were running down pitifully upon her beautiful cheeks'.

An inventory of 1529 records an astonishing list of items used through the liturgical year in this prosperous church, including twelve chalices, a monstrance, a relic, three paxes, two crosses, a pyx, an incense ship, candlesticks and a censer. There was a large collection of vestments:

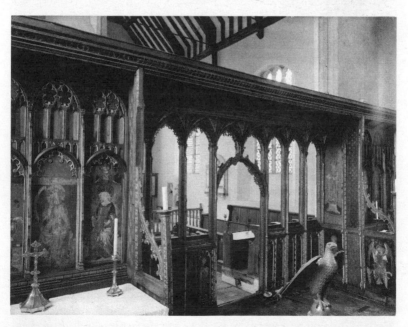

The rood-screen dividing the nave from the chancel at St Helen's, Ranworth, Norfolk, fifteenth century.

A damaged figure of Christ crucified, early
sixteenth century.

thirteen copes and three sets of Mass vestments in crimson, white and
black; there were three coats, two girdles and a selection of jewels to
dress the principal image of the Virgin in the Lady Chapel on great
feast days. The list continues with forty-four altar cloths, eleven Mass
books, six antiphonals, ten grails, fourteen processionals, twenty-one
corporals, a blue silk canopy to bear over the Host at Corpus Christi
and on Palm Sunday, seventeen candlesticks, two holy-water buckets,
two basins, two ewers, two more canopies for the Host, two crosses
and a quantity of streamers, banners and covers. The last include 'A
cloth of Adam and Eve to draw before the High Altar in time of Lent
called the Veil' and three long cloths to hang before the rood-loft

stained or painted with 'the dawnce of Powls' – the Dance of Death.

Martyn's account describes in detail what all of this was used for. The blue silk canopy over the reserved Host, the Sacrament, was carried by four yeomen. On Palm Sunday, when the procession re-enacting Christ's entry into Jerusalem reached the east end of the Lady Chapel, a chorister, attired as an Old Testament prophet, stood on a turret and sang *Ecce Rex tuus venit* (Behold thy King cometh). At this point everyone in the procession knelt. As the Sacrament returned into the church, it was showered with flowers and 'singing cakes', unconsecrated wafers. At Corpus Christi, a feast in celebration of the Eucharist which was universally observed from the fourteenth century, 'they went likewise with the blessed Sacrament in procession about the Church green in Copes'. No other account evokes so vividly what went on in church before the Reformation.

The fourteenth, fifteenth and early sixteenth centuries were the golden age of the parish church; it was the period when it gained a significance that had previously lain with the cathedral. Never again, not even during the Victorian age, was lay enthusiasm and piety to assume such epic proportions. Of the 10,000 or so medieval churches still standing

A rare survival: a mid-fifteenth-century English chasuble re-cut at a later date.

today, between a third and a half were wholly or partly rebuilt during these two and a half centuries.

This was an age of increasing prosperity, particularly through the wool trade, and it was wool fortunes that paid for Long Melford and hundreds of other churches in East Anglia, the Cotswolds and the western counties. The sheer size of some of them amazes us today, looking almost like cathedrals with broad naves and spacious side aisles, timber ceilings soaring above us, and an abundance of glazed windows filling the interior with light. The fact that the new wealth was spent on church building reflected a vigorous lay piety.

The Lateran Council of 1215 had announced that the laity should be educated in the faith. In England it was the Council of Lambeth in 1281 that defined for the first time the role of the laity and stipulated that parishioners should have knowledge of the Ten Commandments, the Seven Works of Mercy, the Seven Virtues, the Seven Deadly Sins and the Seven Sacraments.

Literacy began to spread through the fifteenth century. When by 1500 printing had finally arrived, there was a ready market for every kind of liturgical book, above all Books of Hours, or primers, which were designed for the literate laity to take to church and use during Mass. Their contents varied: they could contain the Seven Penitential Psalms, the Little Office or Hours of the Virgin Mary, the Seven Monastic Hours, the Litany of the Saints, the Office of the Dead, as well as an assortment of prayers to be used at the Elevation of the Host and suffrages to the Virgin. They were, of course, in Latin, and for those who understood the language such literature would have increased their devotion. But fear of Lollardy hindered the use of the vernacular and the translation of the Bible into English. The Lollards were followers of John Wycliffe (c. 1330–84) and opposed the Church's teaching throughout the fifteenth century: they were critical of clerical celibacy, transubstantiation, indulgences and pilgrimages. Moreover, for the Lollards the Bible was the sole authority in all matters of faith;

they held that each man had the right to read and interpret the Scriptures for himself, without the mediation of Church and clergy.

But there was not a total absence of incitements to devotion in the vernacular. Books were published in English instructing worshippers how to behave during Mass, above all the *Lay Folk's Mass Book*, which appeared in several versions, some allegorising and moralising

The elevation of the Host at Mass, from an English primer, fifteenth century.

every step of the liturgy. This was also the age that produced the first indigenous mystics, Richard Rolle (*c.* 1300–49), Walter Hilton (d. 1396) and Julian of Norwich (*c.* 1342–after 1413), and some of their writings became available in English. Works such as Hilton's *Ladder of Perfection*, first printed in English in 1494, Julian's *The Sixteen Revelations of Divine Love* and the anonymous *Cloud of Unknowing* are still read as classics of spirituality today.

Lollardy cast a shadow over two centuries of lay enthusiasm, which expressed itself through communal activities centred on the parish church. Foremost among these were the guilds which proliferated in the late Middle Ages along with the range of their activities. A voluntary association of lay folk, men and women, a guild came together to maintain a particular chapel or altar inside the parish church as the focus of their special devotion. Many of the guilds were dedicated to two new feasts in the Church's calendar, Corpus Christi and the Holy Name. Corpus Christi, officially sanctioned in 1264, took place on the Thursday after Trinity Sunday; the Holy Name became a focus for devotion in the late fifteenth century and in England it was celebrated on 7 August. The guilds were a means whereby ordinary people could live a fuller spiritual life. They maintained lights before a particular image or the Sacrament, staged an annual feast, attended members' funerals and saw that intercessory prayers and Masses were said for the repose of the souls of the departed.

By the early sixteenth century most churches had guilds. In the 1530s in the village of Bressingham in Norfolk, for example, there were two: the first, dedicated to St Peter, was a modest affair supported by the income from two small parcels of land which had been bequeathed in 1460; the other, dedicated to St John the Baptist, was a far wealthier association with a herd of 300 cows, their own chaplain and a separate guildhall. By 1517 that guild was prosperous enough to purchase pardons, or indulgences, for its members.

Indulgences had become important in the late Middle Ages. The pardon obtained was not a remission for a particular sin but of the penance due to God after that sin had been repented, confessed and absolved. In the early Middle Ages the punishment imposed had been hard, but gradually a system of milder penances emerged, involving almsgiving, fasting or spiritual exercises, and what the penitent failed to achieve in full remission of punishment was made up from the treasure of merits acquired by Christ and the saints. The transfer of these merits resided in the power of the pope and the bishops who would grant these indulgences measured in days or years, the most common being forty days. By the late Middle Ages such indulgences were also applied to curtail the torments suffered by the souls in purgatory.

Fear of purgatory and intercession for the dead became central aspects of late medieval religion and explain much about what took place in the parish church. Purgatory was seen as a place between Heaven and Earth where the souls of those who had died in a state of grace received punishment for their sins before they were admitted to Heaven. Capital sins led directly to Hell but minor, or venial, sins could be expurgated either by good works on Earth or by penance in purgatory. In Hell the deceased found themselves in a torture chamber where the smallest pain they endured exceeded the greatest pain on Earth. Punishment fitted the crime: the gluttonous were fed on by toads and serpents; the proud were bound to wheels covered by burning hooks.

The doctrine of purgatory had developed in the twelfth century and found its classic expression in the theology of St Thomas Aquinas (1224–74); it was codified by the Councils of Lyons (1274) and Florence (1439). The Church taught that the souls in purgatory could be helped both by the prayers of the living and by the offering of the Eucharist on their behalf, and every Sunday the priest bade his congregation to pray 'for all soules that abydes the mercy of god in paynes of purgatory'. This led to a proliferation of altars in the form of family or chantry chapels. The term chantry could describe a temporary scheme whereby

Masses were said for the soul of a departed parishioner for a specified period; it could equally denote a small chapel inside the parish church with its own altar and priest – funded by a substantial endowment – whose main purpose it was to say Mass for the soul of the deceased for a much longer period, even in perpetuity. In the fourteenth and fifteenth centuries such permanent chantries multiplied, and the additional clergy assisted the parish priest on Sundays, for instance by providing music.

The average churchgoer would have had a vivid notion of what awaited him after death for it became customary to paint the Doom above or behind the Rood. No one entering the church could escape the vision of the Last Judgement behind the statue of the crucified Christ. Those paintings were whitewashed during the Reformation and very few have survived. In the church of St Peter's at Wenhaston in Suffolk, we can see the outline of the sculpted figures of Christ flanked by Mary and John silhouetted against a crude painting of the Last Judgement. Every such painting spelled out to the faithful what would happen on the Last Day when Christ would come to judge the living and the dead – not on the basis of their profession of piety but by their actions in life.

Although on entering the church the eye would have been drawn to the dominant images of the Rood and Doom, the building was, at ground level, polycentric – divided into separate areas of varying sizes which were partitioned from each other. There were various chapels and altars, and the overall effect would have been of flickering lights drawing the eye to this or that particular area, whether to adore the Host suspended in the pyx over the High Altar or to seek the intercession of a saint at a side chapel. Bishop Alcock of Ely thus described the parish church as 'Everyman's Bethlehem'. Private pews became commonplace in the fifteenth century – and provided the church with additional income – and parishioners now specified in their wills that they wished to be buried close to where they sat each Sunday, 'afore my seat'. Consequently the

Doom painting, St Peter and St Paul, Chaldon, Surrey, fifteenth century.

once open space in the centre of the church began to be filled with the pews and tombs of the wealthy.

Images of saints were omnipresent, many parish churches paying respect to local figures, such as St Thomas Cantilupe in Herefordshire or St Richard in Gloucestershire. Their images were painted on the walls, carved on the ceiling in the form of bosses or in tiers of statues on a reredos, or displayed as separate objects of devotion at particular altars. In addition armies of angels would spread their wings, often gilded, across the hammer-beam roofs of many a perpendicular church. Thus the parishioners were reassured by the presence of an array of mediators between Earth and Heaven whose prayers they sought. No aspect of daily life was devoid of its heavenly intercessor: St Christopher assisted travellers, St Sebastian protected against the plague, St Erasmus's help was sought for stomach disorders and St Apollonia's for toothache.

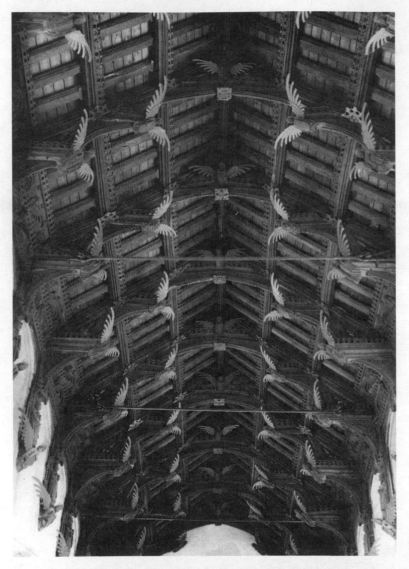

The heavenly host, St Wendreda, March, Cambridgeshire, fifteenth century.

Yet the greatest reverence was accorded the Virgin: her image over the entrance porch welcomed the worshipper and inside the church her portrait was omnipresent. The greatest gathering of holy intercessors, however, would adorn the rood-screen.

The church of St Helen's at Ranworth in Norfolk, hidden amid the fastnesses of the broads, is the most remarkable survival. Its rood-screen gives an unforgettable impression of the richness that was swept away by the Reformation. The colours are sumptuous and there is an abundance of flowery patterns and gilding. It is flanked, on either side, by chapels, each held in by a parclose screen. The first chapel is dedicated to a variety of saints: St Felix, who brought Christianity to East Anglia; St George, the patron of England, popular after the victory of Agincourt, trampling the dragon underfoot; St Etheldreda, abbess

Alabaster statue of the Virgin and Child, fifteenth century.

of nearby Ely; and St Barbara, patron of soldiers, gunsmiths and fire-fighters, whose name was invoked against accidents and sudden death. The Lady Chapel, on the other side of the rood-screen, is dedicated to childbirth, and motherhood is represented in the four panels over the altar. Painted in the middle of the fifteenth century, the rendering of these saints reflects the humanity at the heart of late medieval devotion: for all the richness of their robes these are women with toddlers with whom any parishioner could easily identify.

Church interiors add to our knowledge of what occupied the medieval mind. Both windows and walls could be given over to catechising the congregation with sequences depicting the whole cycle of the Gospel. The chancel of St Mary's at Chalgrove in Oxfordshire has one of the most complete of the cycles that survive, painted in red, yellow and black and dating from the mid-fourteenth century. Panels on the pulpits often depicted the Four Latin Doctors of the Church – St Ambrose, St Augustine, St Gregory and St Jerome – to remind the congregation of those who had created the framework of the Christian faith. In East Anglia there was a fashion for what is known as seven-sacrament fonts, which illustrate baptism, confirmation, marriage, penance, ordination, extreme unction and the Eucharist.

Medieval Christians fervently believed in the power of the in-animate to protect and ward off evil. Holy water, in particular, was a powerful agent. The salt and water in the baptismal font and that used for the asperges, or sprinkling, at High Mass were administered with repeated crossings to cast out demons: 'let every delusion and wickedness, and every craftiness of devilish cunning, scatter and depart when called upon'. The holy water used in the asperges could be taken home, like the candles blessed at Candlemas, to ward off the forces of darkness. Holy words and gestures too had power to dispel evil. Sometimes, as in the case of prayers to St Michael and the angels, the practice came close to magic with the prayers resembling incantations.

The holy water used for baptism was locked up in the font at the

The Christian story told on the church walls, St Mary, Chalgrove, Oxfordshire, fourteenth century.

west end of the church. Baptism also accounts for the increasing elaboration of porches throughout the Middle Ages. Nowadays the church
porch is little more than a repository for notices of times of services
or the flower rota, but in medieval times it was the setting for major
rites of passage. Baptism took place within days of birth, the baby being
borne to the church by the midwife and the godparents. The priest met
them in the porch and having asked the sex of the child, placed a boy
to the right and a girl to the left. The baptismal party would bring along
salt for the first exorcism; some of it was placed in the child's mouth
and prayers said, after which the infant's forehead was signed twice with
a cross. After spitting into his left hand the priest moistened the child's
ears and nostrils in emulation of similar actions by Christ when healing

the deaf and dumb man. He then made the sign of the cross on the child's right hand: 'May you remain in the Catholic faith and have eternal life for ever and ever. Amen.' Invited by the priest to 'Go into the temple of God', the party now entered the church and gathered round the font. On behalf of the baby the godparents renounced Satan and all his works, and the priest, after dipping his thumb into holy oil, signed him with the cross on his breast and on his back between the shoulder blades. Stripped bare and with his head turned east and his face north, the child was rotated three times and each time plunged completely in the font, in rhythmic response to the words 'God the Father, God the Son and the Holy Spirit'. A senior godparent then lifted the child out of the font and the infant was signed by the priest on the top of his head with the most holy of oils, chrism. The baby was then put into its chrisom, a piece of cloth or hooded robe covering head and body, which the child had to wear until it was returned to the priest by the mother attending the churching ceremony. A lighted candle was then placed in the infant's right hand to the words, 'Receive a burning and inextinguishable light', after which the godparents were enjoined to bring the child up in the Christian faith.

This rite explains the increasing elaboration of the font, resulting in miniature Gothic skyscrapers soaring almost up into the roof timbers and calling for hoists to lift them. But the font also played an important part in the rite of confirmation, which could be undergone at any age, largely because bishops were often unavailable to perform the ceremony. Using chrism the bishop signed the candidate on the forehead with the sign of the cross, after which it was bandaged. Between three and eight days later the candidate would return to church where the bandage was removed and burnt and his forehead washed in the font.

Apart from baptism, the porch also played an important role in the rite of churching. It was here that the priest greeted the mother – forty days after the birth of a boy and eighty days after the birth of a girl – and after prayers and a sprinkling with holy water, he led

Porch, St Mary, Radwinter, Essex, fourteenth century.

her and a party of women friends into the church to return the chrisom cloth and make a monetary offering. Finally, the porch was the place where a large part of the medieval marriage ceremony took place – a fact so memorably captured in Chaucer's Wife of Bath: 'She'd had five husbands, all at the church door.'

But everything about the medieval village church focused on the community of the living and the dead. Everywhere the eye would have been caught by the names of dead donors with the exhortation to pray for them. Most important was the bede-roll. Before the offertory at High Mass came the bidding prayers, 'the bidding of the bedes', a roll call of the beads that embraced the pope, the clergy, the king, the lords and commons, the local authorities, the parish and particularly any in need of remembrance. The congregation then prayed for the souls of deceased parishioners and benefactors. Once a year the entire bede-roll was read at a parish requiem, where those present were asked to remember all those who in centuries past had been members of the congregation and benefactors to the church. No other ceremony illustrates so potently the sacred space of the parish church, serving as the repository of the collective memory of the community.

In the parish church the redemption of the world was re-enacted every Sunday through the mystery of the Mass. This was the moment when the whole parish came together, kneeling and raising their eyes in adoration at the sound of the sacring bell. Devotion to the Eucharist was central to late medieval piety and to see the elevated Host was in itself a blessing. Occasionally squint holes appear in rood-screens for this very purpose. The custom of lifting up the Host had originated in France in the early thirteenth century, and the Elevation took place immediately after the words of consecration, *Hoc est enim Corpus Meum*, when candles and torches were lit. So important was this central part of the Mass that in churches with elaborate altars a cloth was drawn across it so that the Host could be clearly seen silhouetted against it.

The Mass could be celebrated either in its simple form as a Low Mass, or as a Solemn or High Mass, involving more clergy, grander ceremonies and singing. Its basic structure, however, was immutable. The ceremony began with the Confiteor, or confession, by the priest, followed by the opening prayer or collect, the Epistle, Gospel and, in the High Mass, the Creed. Then came the offertory, the offering of money, followed by the consecration of bread and wine. The prayer of consecration culminating in the

John Waymont and his wife at the feet of St Jerome and St Ambrose
entreat the passer-by to pray for their souls, St Thomas, Foxley, Norfolk.

Elevation of the Host completed the set liturgy of the Mass and was followed by the Lord's Prayer. Just before taking communion the priest kissed the corporal on which the consecrated Host lay, then the lip of the chalice, and afterwards the pax, a disc or tablet of precious material on which there was depicted a sacred emblem like an *Agnus Dei* or a crucifix. Most Sundays the people did not receive communion and the pax was then kissed by the congregation, in order of rank; this was a substitute for what in earlier times had been an actual kiss and today takes the form of a handshake. The Mass ended with the blessing, dismissal and the distribution of the Holy Loaf, which like the kissing of the pax served as a substitute for communion. Each Sunday parishioners took their turn in baking the bread, and bringing it to church, where they presented it to the priest along with a lit candle. The priest solemnly blessed the bread and the Holy Loaf was then cut up and distributed to the congregation.

The atmosphere in church must have been quite boisterous at times and, bearing in mind that matins and Mass could last some three hours, it is likely that people came and went as they still do during the service in the Orthodox Church. William Caxton complains in his *Doctrinal of Sapience*, the translation of a French pastoral work published in 1486, that around the lesser altars people would jostle and misbehave while Mass was in progress, 'in spekyng, in lawhing and many other maners'. An early Tudor poem reminded people that the church is 'a place of prayer / not of claterynge and talkynge ... charge them also to keepe theyr sight in the chirche close upon theyr bokes / stande or syt / and never to walk in the chirche'. The Mass should be heard 'qyuetly and devoutly / moche parte knelynge'. But 'at the gospel at the preface / and at the Pater Noster teche them to stande / and to make curtsy at this worde Jesus as the preest dothe'.

Communion was taken once a year, at Easter. It was referred to as 'taking one's rights' and everyone over the age of fourteen was bound by law to receive it. The communicant had to prepare for the sacrament by an act of penance or confession, so that he should be 'arayde in Godys lyvere, clothyd in love and charyte'. This penance could be a brusque

A wooden pax, *c.* 1500.

affair with the priest listing off to the kneeling penitent the Seven Deadly
Sins, the Five Senses and the Seven Works of Mercy. But through confession the priest was often able to settle disputes within the village community and enforce an overall morality on his flock. The Host was received
at the rood-screen, and stretched across each communicant's hands was
the so-called houselling cloth, a strip of fabric designed to catch any
crumbs that might fall by accident. Communion was taken in only one

kind, but a draught of unconsecrated wine was handed to communicants with which to wash down the Host.

In addition to Sunday Mass parish life was structured by the events of the liturgical year, which oscillated between fast and feast days. Some, such as Christmas and saints' days, were fixed; others moved, including Easter, Pentecost (Whit Sunday) and Corpus Christi. Alongside the great feasts of the Trinity season – the Transfiguration of Christ (6 August), the Assumption of the Virgin (15 August), All Saints (1 November) and All Souls (2 November) – there were celebrations of local saints and feasts of the various guilds.

The liturgical year opened with Candlemas (2 February), which marked the end of the Christmas season. During the feast, commemorating the presentation of the Christ child in the temple, candles were blessed and distributed; they were deemed to have power against inimical forces: 'wherever it shall be lit or set up, the devil may flee away in fear and trembling with all his ministers'. All the great feasts were marked by processions in which everyone took part. Rogationtide, the solemn beating of the parish bounds on 25 April, could last several days depending on the size of the parish. This was a ceremony designed to drive out evil spirits, invoke blessings on the coming harvest and, at the same time, define the village community. Handbells were rung and the procession carried many crosses and banners, one of them showing a dragon with a long tail which, on the last day, was cut off to signal the defeat of the devil.

The climax of the year, however, was Holy Week, beginning with Palm Sunday. Branches of yew, box and willow were sprinkled with holy water and distributed, and the whole village, ranked in hierarchical order, made its way to the stone cross that stood in the churchyard, usually on the north side. Here they were met by the ecclesiastical procession, carrying relics and the Host under a canopy. At the cross the story of Christ's entry into Jerusalem was read from Matthew's

Gospel, and as the congregation approached, singers, often dressed as Old Testament prophets, would sing 'Behold thy King cometh', at which point everyone knelt and venerated the Sacrament. The two processions now merged and together wound their way around the east end to the south side of the church. There choristers, sited on a stage, greeted their arrival with 'All glory, laud and honour to Thee Redeemer King'. As the Sacrament passed by it was showered with flowers and 'singing cakes'. Finally the procession reached the west door, which only opened after the priest knocked at it with the foot of the processional cross. Both the relics and the Host were lifted on high allowing the procession to pass beneath them into the church. As the Sacrament made its entry a veil that had hidden the Rood was withdrawn and the *Ave Rex Noster* sung. As we know from Roger Martyn's account, during the Mass that followed, the Passion narrative from Matthew's Gospel was sung from the gallery beneath the Rood.

On Maundy Thursday, the day of the Last Supper and the institution of the Eucharist, a Solemn Mass was celebrated in which three Hosts were consecrated: one for the priest's communion that day, another for his communion on Good Friday and a third for placing in the Easter Sepulchre. At the close of this Mass all altars were stripped and washed down with wine and water. Good Friday was observed as a day of mourning, which saw the congregation arriving barefoot in penitence. They listened to the Passion narrative from the Gospel of John, and when the passage describing the parting of Christ's garments was read, two linen cloths were taken from the altar. The Reproaches were then sung during which a veiled cross was exposed in three stages, each one marked by the words: 'Behold the wood of the cross on which hung the saviour of the world, come, let us worship.' One by one the clergy and the congregation came forward on their knees, to kiss the exposed crucifix. After communion vespers were said, and the priest laid the pyx, containing the remaining consecrated Host together with a cross wrapped in a linen cloth, into the Easter Sepulchre. The

The Easter Sepulchre at St Patrick, Patrington, Humberside, fifteenth century. The carved tomb is divided into four tiers. On the lowest we see the sleeping soldiers of the Passion story, dressed as medieval knights; the next tier contains the niche into which the cross and the Host were placed; and further up we see the figure of Christ, his hand raised in benediction, arising from the tomb flanked by two censing angels. The empty space at the top must once have contained a relief of the Ascension.

Sepulchre stood on the north side of the chancel and could be a temporary structure of wood, or a combination of wood and stone, like that put up on the benefactor's altar tomb at Long Melford. During the fifteenth century, however, it began to take on permanent form, and one magnificent example has survived in St Patrick's church at Patrington on Humberside.

Holy Week reached its climax at Mass on Easter Sunday. The Host was retrieved from the Easter Sepulchre and placed in the pyx suspended over the High Altar. The crucifix was raised and carried in triumph around the church to the ringing of bells and the singing of *Christus resurgens*. It was then laid on an altar and once again venerated by clergy and congregation approaching on their knees.

All these ceremonies of the Christian year brought constant animation to the church building and reflected a faith with a strong sense of theatre. Through them both individual piety and collective identity found their expression and permeated everyday life. Moreover, the many rituals that took place in the parish church impinged on every single person from cradle to grave, beginning with baptism at the font, through confirmation, marriage and the churching of women after childbirth, to extreme unction and, finally, burial.

But we must remember that religious life was also permeated with popular superstition: religion often slipped over towards magic. As consecrated spaces the church and the churchyard were deemed to possess power to ward off evil. Special significance was attributed to the churchyard soil, and if a churchyard was violated by crime, a special act of reconciliation was necessary before it could be used again. The key to the church door was supposed to be effective against mad dogs, and as the church bells were also consecrated, they were efficacious against evil spirits and would be rung to dispel thunder and lightning for which demons were held responsible. The Church tolerated a whole world of popular superstition, ranging from amulets in shape of the *Agnus Dei*, thought to be effective against storms, death in childbirth, fire and drowning, to the use of holy water and holy bread for medicinal purposes.

A seemingly endless series of baptisms, marriages and burials would have been performed in the parish church. For a burial, vespers for the dead were recited in the church the previous night. On the day itself the service included the Dirige, matins with readings from the Book of Job and the Requiem Mass. For the wealthy this solitary requiem was but a prelude to a series of votive Masses for the repose of the deceased's soul and its release from the pains of purgatory. One very popular sequence was known as the Trental of St Gregory and consisted of thirty Masses spread over a year, with three being celebrated on each of the principal feasts of Christ and the Virgin.

Sermons, however, were rare – a fact that accounts for the paucity of medieval pulpits. Instead, four times a year, the incumbent expounded the fundamentals of the faith in the vernacular: the fourteen articles of faith, the Ten Commandments, the two precepts of the Gospels, the Seven Works of Mercy, the Seven Deadly Sins, the Seven Virtues and the Seven Sacraments.

But what kind of man was the village priest? Medieval clergy were an uneven bunch – which might equally be said of clergy at any

A priest celebrates Mass, fourteenth century.

A priest gives communion,
fourteenth century.

time – and fell into two distinct groups: prosperous rectors and poor
vicars. As the right of presentation lay in the main with the local lord
of the manor, it was usually bestowed on a younger son, who took
most of the income and put in place a poorly paid vicar. The latter
came from the labouring classes, usually a likely lad who began as a
server and then moved on to become what was known as the holy-
water clerk: someone who looked after the church, could read the epistle,
do the responses at Mass and carry the holy-water bucket. This would
have brought sufficient income to enable him to get private tuition or
attend the local grammar school; all that was required of a vicar was
a working knowledge of written and spoken Latin. He would then
become a parson living on a stipend from an absentee rector or a
monastery that had the right of presentation and chose to hang on to
the majority of the church's income.

But the vicar had to engender enough income to pay for an assistant and, often as not, support a mistress, which he made through
letting – or farming himself – the glebe land belonging to the church.
In addition he was entitled to the tithe, which was divided into the
great tithe coming in the form of cattle and crops, and the lesser tithe,
which was applied to everything else the village produced, such as
eggs, vegetables and fruit. But in many cases the rector would take

the great tithe, leaving the vicar with only the lesser. Finally, he could also draw on the altarage, a monetary contribution that was made when a parishioner received communion or was buried. We must remember that the incumbent's commitments were substantial, for he was responsible for the upkeep of the fabric of the chancel, had to pay any assistant clergy and to give alms and hospitality to the needy.

The fourteenth and fifteenth centuries also reveal the importance of churchwardens – whose role had been created in 1129 at the Council of London – for we have the first surviving accounts from that period. Generally two wardens were elected annually – women were not excluded – who were responsible for the fabric of the main body of the church, for its security (it was locked at night) and for the provision of all the items needed to maintain the liturgy, including the cleaning, repair and replacement of vestments. Often they would have deputies, called light wardens, whose task it was to maintain the lights in the church and look after the store of candles. The churchwardens' responsibility also extended to the maintenance of the churchyard, including seeing that anyone whose animals grazed on it was prosecuted. In the case of a major building project, their financial responsibility would have been considerable. They had to pay both the parish clerk and the sexton and to keep the accounts. In addition, they were in charge of the poor relief. Money, therefore, had to be raised and, although there might be a levy on the parish, it was most likely to come from the sale of church ales. The churchwardens bought in large amounts of malt which was brewed into ale; it was a virtual norm that each church had its brew house. At certain festive periods of the year there would be a church-ale sale, in effect a parish drinking party, the proceeds of which helped maintain the church.

The cycle of late medieval village life must have seemed immutable. Even the dead remained close to the living for they were buried either under the church floor or in the churchyard. Grand tombs began to appear, made of stone or Purbeck marble, with recumbent effigies of the deceased in all the glory of their rank. Initially the carved lids of stone coffins remained exposed on the church floor – the earliest of these date from the twelfth century – but they soon multiplied and developed into the effigy upon a raised chest, to which a canopy was later added. The late Middle Ages then saw the introduction of the incised stone slab and the monumental brass. While these grand tombs were only affordable to the wealthy, in the fifteenth century more and more people invested in a memorial of some kind in their parish church. In addition, chantry chapels along with coats of arms and donor portraits in windows asserted the lordly presence as never before within the church building.

From both rich and poor, however, came the cry with which I started this chapter: 'Pray for my soul . . .' But although no one in 1530 could have predicted that within three decades it would be gone, time was running out for this world. Roger Martyn was to rescue what he could of the glories of Long Melford, including the altarpiece from the family chapel, 'a table with a crucifix on it, with the two thieves hanging, on every side, one which is in my House decayed, and the same I hope my heiress will repair, and restore again, one day'. Alas, that day was never to come.

Chapter 3

Obedience

ST MARY'S CHURCH AT FAIRFORD in Gloucestershire was consecrated in 1497, only three decades before the great cataclysm of the Reformation. It is a monument to the vigour of the Church and of its laity in the late fifteenth century and, in Fairford's case, to one man, the wool merchant John Tame. Tame died in 1500, three years on from the dedication of St Mary's, bequeathing censers and cross, candlesticks and cruets, all made of silver, together with vestments and the sum of £240 for the foundation of a chantry. In his will he wrote: 'First I bequeathe my sowle to Almighty God, and our Blissid Lady, and to alle the blissid saints in hevin, and my body to be buried in the Northe Chapell of the Church of Our Lady at Fayreford.' Beneath the brasses of himself and his wife runs the following verse:

For thus love pray for me,
I may not pray nowe praye ye
With A pater noster and an ave
That my paynys Relessyd may be.

Fairford's glory are its twenty-eight stained-glass windows, amounting to over 2,000 square feet of glass. Their subject matter, which presents the entire Catholic faith in visual form, is lifted from the woodcuts of the hugely popular picture Bible, the *Biblia Pauperum*. The windows show the stories of the Old Testament: Eve in the Garden of Eden, Moses and the burning bush, Gideon and the golden fleece, and King Solomon and the queen of Sheba. Appropriately the windows at the high altar end of the church depict scenes from the life of Christ; at the west end appear the four Evangelists; and the four Latin doctors of the Church can be seen on either side of the nave. The chronology

St Mary, Fairford, Gloucestershire.

of the biblical story is only interrupted in the case of the central light of the east window, which depicts the Assumption of the Virgin to whom the church is dedicated. Other windows show prophets and apostles, martyrs and enemies of the faith.

John Tame may have paid for the church but evidence suggests that the splendid and costly windows were a gift from the first Tudor, Henry VII, lord of the Fairford estates, and the work of his glazier, Bernard Flower. This might partly explain why the glass and other things later survived the assault of the iconoclasts. But in addition to the royal connection we should consider the role played by the benefactor's son, Sir Edmund Tame, who must have guarded the church and protected what he could during the tempestuous middle years of the sixteenth century; in Gloucestershire, under the rabidly Protestant Bishop Hooper, the ravages were more vicious than elsewhere. To the son too we surely owe the rare survival of a complete set of choir and parclose screens, fittings for which Bishop Hooper had a particular dislike. High up, the angel corbels would have been out of the easy reach of image breakers. Surprisingly, inside the porch the image of the Virgin too has survived, and on the west side of the tower, we still see one of the most popular of all late medieval devotional icons, the Image of Pity, depicting the resurrected Christ with his right hand raised in blessing and displaying on his left the Resurrection Cross.

At Fairford we gain a rare glimpse into a spiritual world on the verge of being blown away in the tempest of the Reformation. No one was to escape this storm, neither high nor low, neither rich nor poor: all were to be engulfed by a bewildering tide of events that cut through the very fabric of their everyday lives. One year the faithful would be exhorted to go on a pilgrimage to venerate the relics of a saint, as described in Chaucer's *Canterbury Tales*; the next the shrine would be levelled to the ground and carts would carry away its treasures. One Holy Week the Easter Sepulchre would be erected in the church; the next it would be prohibited. One year the images of saints would have votive candles flickering before them and then, suddenly, such lights were forbidden, followed, not long after, by the destruction of the images themselves.

For the majority of the population the Reformation was what happened to their local parish church, which was to change radically both in appearance and in what took place within its walls. It was to be a long, drawn-out process lasting more than a century. For the people who lived through its two most turbulent phases, 1547 to 1570 and 1640 to 1660, the impact must have been traumatic. But while in the latter phase we hear about the effect of events on ordinary people who by then had found a voice, this is not the case during the first cataclysm, which tore apart the rhythm of everyday life and piety that had evolved over more than a thousand years. We know today that the Reformation had no popular roots: it was not a response to demands from below. On the contrary, it was savagely imposed from above on a people who had been nurtured on the notion that obedience to the powers-that-be was a prime principle of life. The great silence that surrounds this dramatic event remains one of English history's greatest mysteries.

No one could have predicted that when Henry VIII embarked on seeking a divorce from his wife, Katherine of Aragon, in the interests of marrying again to produce a male heir, this would lead to such a disruption of ordinary lives. At the outset, what was happening in London had little effect on what took place in the thousands of country churches and chapels dotted across Tudor England. Indeed, it is striking how slowly the erosion of traditional religion progressed in its initial phases. In 1533 the Act in Restraint of Appeals abolished papal authority, substituting the king for the pope. The latter was to disappear from parish prayers, an alteration so slight as to be unnoticeable. But at the centre of power, those at court who supported the assault on the Catholic Church initiated by Martin Luther in Germany began to campaign against the fabric of traditional spirituality. Pilgrimages, the cult of the saints, purgatory, intercession for the dead, pardons, the use of votive candles and the proliferation of holy days were all attacked. Yet in the countryside people would at the most have heard news of the divorce of the king's first queen and then his subsequent marriages, first to Anne Boleyn, by whom he had a daughter, Elizabeth, and then to Jane Seymour who, in 1536, produced the long-awaited male heir, Edward.

It was in that year that the ordinary churchgoer would have begun to experience the radical phase of the Reformation. First, they would have seen all monastic houses within their locality dissolved, their monks and nuns dispersed, their contents confiscated by the Crown and carried away in carts, and the buildings dismantled for their materials and left to decay. What was left became a useful quarry for the new owner of the land, who also took over the right of presentation to any benefices that the monastery had once held.

Far more significant was a revision in the observance of holy days. In the late Middle Ages there had been some fifty of them, but suddenly in 1536 all feasts between 1 July and 29 September were abolished, apparently for interfering with the gathering of the harvest: such days took men and women off the fields when they should have been working the land. So were all those feasts which fell in the Westminster law terms, for they hindered government administration. The only exceptions were the feasts of the Apostles, the Virgin, Ascension Day, the nativity of John the Baptist, All Saints and Candlemas. The abolition of the holy days triggered off some unrest but, for the most part, it appears that the directive was simply ignored; most parishes went on celebrating their local saints as they always had.

In 1536 the first doctrinal statement of the new Church of England, the Ten Articles, signalled no dramatic change but bore signs of what was to come. Only three of the seven sacraments were upheld – baptism, penance and the Eucharist. The intercession of the saints could still be sought, but the clergy were to warn their congregations of the danger of worshipping images, 'censing them, and kneeling and offering unto them'. Despite warnings against idolatry no one as yet questioned the place and legitimacy of images as such.

A series of injunctions issued in August 1536 by the king's vicar general in ecclesiastical affairs, Thomas Cromwell, were far more overtly reformist. Clerics were to encourage their parishioners to read the Bible in Latin and English, and to preach to their flocks on the Ten Articles. Fathers and landlords were to catechise their families and households on the Lord's Prayer, the Creed and the Ten Commandments. In 1538 a second set of injunctions went a good deal further. Parishes were now instructed to purchase Miles Coverdale's English translation of the Bible, which was to be made freely available to all. The saints were largely excised from the litany, the use of the rosary condemned and the ringing of the angelus bell forbidden. All shrines in the great places of pilgrimage like Canterbury and Durham were to be demolished, the relics destroyed and any treasure confiscated by the Crown. The faithful were exhorted not to go 'wandering to pilgrimages, offering of money, candles or tapers to images or relics, or kissing or licking the same'. A further step was taken when any 'feigned images', which evoked such responses, were ordered to be taken down. This went hand in hand with the abolition of 'candles, tapers, or images of wax ... before any image or picture'. This single injunction set in train the destruction of church interiors, which were gradually dismantled over the next thirty years. Here starts the snuffing out of the lights, the wiping out of an atmosphere that was only to be restored, to some churches, three centuries later.

A further set of injunctions that year introduced another requirement which continues to this day: '... the curate of every parish church shall keep one book or register, which book he shall, every Sunday take forth and in the presence of the churchwardens or one of them, write and record in the same all the weddings, christenings and burials made the whole week before'. The parish register was a revolutionary innovation and the first step towards making both incumbent and parish

The parish chest, St Oswald, Lower Peover, Cheshire, fifteenth century.

officers agents of the state. The register was to be kept in a locked chest within the church; even today many can still to be found tucked away in odd corners of churches.

Thus by the end of the 1530s ordinary parishioners would have felt the hand of change, particularly if their local bishop supported the reforms. Nicholas Shaxton, bishop of Salisbury, was such a cleric who waged a war against relics, demanding that they be taken out of any church and delivered to him for destruction. Money which had been raised for candles, he dictated, was to be used for buying the English Bible. In Kent, where those sympathetic to the Reformation had gained a strong foothold, images were smashed, although, as yet, there was no official directive. At court the passion for change ebbed and flowed as the king moved first in one direction and then in another, finally adopting a conservative stance when traditional teaching was reinstated in the Six Articles of 1539. These maintained the Roman view of clerical celibacy, transubstantiation, communion in one kind and auricular confession. At the same time the architect of the Reformation in England, Thomas Cromwell, fell from power. Many ordinary churchgoers must have thought that this was as far as the reforms would go. In fact, it was just the calm before the storm.

Early in 1547, within weeks of the accession of the nine-year-old Edward, the storm broke. A new set of injunctions set out to alter every church in the kingdom and what took place within it. All images were to be destroyed, all processions were to cease, even the one that preceded the Sunday Mass; instead, the cleric was bidden to kneel and read the litany, an English version of which had been introduced by the reformist archbishop of Canterbury, Thomas Cranmer, in 1544. There was to be no holy water or holy bread and the use of votive candles was forbidden. Money which had been raised for these by the various chantries, guilds and fraternities was to go into the poor box. Then, in December 1547, before these institutions could offer any

significant resistance, they too were suppressed, with the Crown confiscating their goods, lands and income.

The importance of these corporations to the parish church has
only in recent years been fully explored and appreciated. They had
taken on major responsibilities in the running of the church, for
example through raising money for expansion or repairs, and with
their suppression an important source of income disappeared. So too
did an important link binding the living and the dead, as the major
purpose of their work had been to intercede for the souls of the
deceased. Their abolition started a process that denied that the living
could exercise influence on behalf of the dead; with it went the priests
whose function it had been to say Requiem Masses. In the larger parish
churches, the guilds and fraternities had also been responsible for the
efflorescence of music. This now became the responsibility of a single
clerk who might at best co-opt those in the parish who were able to
sing. In many places music ceased altogether.

A visitation of the entire country took place in 1547–8, conducted
by no less than thirty commissioners, men who in their zeal went far
beyond what the injunctions had ordered. We get a glimpse of what
happened in the account of Robert Parkyn, a priest at Adwick le Street
near Doncaster. He recorded how all the images were taken away, all
the lights snuffed bar one on the altar, how none of the traditional
ceremonies at Candlemas, Ash Wednesday, Palm Sunday and Good
Friday were performed. Nor was there an Easter Sepulchre, the
Rogationtide procession was abrogated, and churchyard crosses began
to be smashed. Holy bread and water were abolished and, as Parkyn
recorded with some anguish, 'Yea, & also the pixes hangynge over thal-
ters (wherin was remaynyng Christ blesside bode under forme of
breade) was dispitt fully cast away as thinges most abominable ...'
These words capture something of the shock and sense of violation
which all this must have caused in parish after parish.

In the spring of 1548 a licence to preach was introduced, intended to give control to the state over what was said in the pulpit; it was to remain in place until the outbreak of the Civil War in 1642. Devoid of such a licence the incumbent was to read instead to his congregation one of the approved homilies (to which I will return later). But religious controversy had become so heated that by the autumn of that year the government banned sermons altogether.

At Whitsun 1549, the Book of Common Prayer was introduced. It was to be the first of several such Prayer Books – a second, more radical version appeared in 1552 and a third, revised version in 1559; there were to be later modifications in 1604 and 1662. But it was not until the 1580s that the Book of Common Prayer was generally accepted, and I will therefore deal with the services it introduced, and which were to remain in use until the twentieth century, in detail in the next chapter. The Prayer Book of 1549 swept away any variant celebrations of the Mass, replacing it with a ceremony in the vernacular that was stripped of all the traditional externals such as holy bread and water, 'bidding the beads' and the elevation of the Host. The service remained, as had the old Latin Mass, non-participatory except for one major change: at Communion everyone was to receive both bread and wine. The Prayer Book also reduced the traditional liturgical year to Christmas, Easter, Whitsun and a handful of saints' days.

It is remarkable that we have no record of the impact of this revolutionary change on the ordinary communicant. Yet with the reforms a whole framework of life was swept away. As a consequence there were disturbances in the West Midlands and in Yorkshire, but by far the most serious was the rebellion the reforms triggered in the South-west. Here the introduction of the Prayer Book was seen as the last straw in a series of depredations that included the enclosure of land by greedy landlords. Riot and commotion erupted in the villages of Cornwall and Devon, and in July a peasant army appeared outside the walls of Exeter, demanding a reversal of the reforms. The rebellion was brutally put down by foreign mercenaries. Four thousand were killed and priests in particular were singled out for cruel treatment; one was left to die of exposure chained to his church tower, robed in his Mass vestments and festooned with a holy-water bucket, sprinkler, sacring bell, rosary and 'other lyke popyshe trash'.

But it appears that on the whole, like it or not, people obediently went along with the changes. Early in 1550 the reformers went one step further and ordered 'the defacing of images and the bringing in of books of old Service in the Church'. All of these things were to be gathered together and destroyed. In a diocese like Gloucester with its radical bishop, John Hooper, who arrived in 1551, the effect could be devastating. The visitation articles of that year enquired of every parish whether the incumbent's teaching and preaching were based on the Scriptures and whether justification by faith alone was expounded; it checked that prayers were addressed only to God and not to any saint, that no adoration of the Sacrament took place and that the Bible was both read and heard. It continued with an instruction to

> ... take doune and remove out of their churches and chapels
> ... [all] tabernacles, tombes, sepulchres, tables, footstools,
> rood-lofts, and such other monuments, signs, tokens,
> reliques, leavings, and remembrances, where such supersti-
> tion, idols, images, or other provocation of idolatry have
> been used ... And to take doune all the chappells, closets,
> partitions, and separations within ... [their] churches,
> whereas any masse hath been said, or idol, image or relique
> used to be honoured.

They were to 'take doun and abolish all altars' and set up 'the Lords Board', in effect a wooden dining table. The parishioners were to learn by rote the Ten Commandments, and they were not to make use of Latin primers and rosaries. If there was anything left in the church

Defaced images, St Peter, Ringland, Norfolk.

after this onslaught, the government ordered its confiscation in March 1551 to help pay for the war with Scotland.

Then, in 1552, the second Prayer Book implemented a complete break with the past. As I shall describe in more detail later, it introduced a communion service in which both cleric and congregation participated together. With the exception of the surplice all vestments were forbidden. The Holy Table, which replaced the altar, was to be moved into the body of the chancel and placed in a north–south position for communion, for which the word Mass was finally dropped. Any notion that the Eucharist represented the sacrifice of Christ on the cross had disappeared: the communion service was purely commemorative – something that was emphasised in the instruction that any of the consecrated bread or wine left over should be taken and consumed at home. Anointing, which was traditional at baptism, ordination, confirmation and during the visiting of the sick, also ceased; so did the reservation of the Sacrament, even for carrying it to give communion to the dying. And as to 'touching, kneeling, crossing, holding up of hands, knocking upon the breast, and other gestures, they may be used or left, as every man's devotion serveth, without blame'.

Any notion that the living could act on behalf of the departed had also disappeared: the funeral service read as though the corpse was absent, the priest instead addressing the mourners. In a huge break with the past, where the focus had been on releasing the departed from the pains of purgatory through Requiem Masses and prayer, the laity was now told that these practices were meaningless and had no effect. The dead were savagely cut off from the living; not even a simple prayer could help them. This rejection of previous beliefs must have been devastating for many.

When Edward VI had come to the throne in 1547, churches had been filled with devotional objects and items essential for the perform-ance of the liturgy. The church had been a compartmented space filled with nooks and corners partitioned off for a variety of altars or frater-nities. The eye was held and guided by the presence of flickering lights illuminating numerous images. By the close of 1552 the church had become one large, empty, whitewashed enclosure. Colour, which had

The destruction of traditional religion, from John Foxe, *Actes and Monuments*, 1563.

been everywhere, on the walls, the polychrome statues, the vestments and the altar dressings, had vanished. So had the smell of incense. All that the church was left with was a surplice, two tablecloths for the Holy Table, a communion cup and a bell to ring before the sermon.

The new service aimed to restore the Eucharist to the centre of the community by rendering it into the vernacular and giving both the bread and wine to worshippers on a regular basis. But we have no way of knowing whether this actually happened. Did a great number of people communicate every Sunday? The reformers had replaced the drama of the Mass, culminating in the elevation of the Host, with something that lacked colourful ceremonial and attempted instead an archaeological reconstruction of the Last Supper. A highly cerebral religion of the Word was suddenly imposed on congregations where most could not read. At the close of the century, the great Elizabethan theologian of the Church of England, Richard Hooker, realised what had been lost and pointed to the importance of outward appearances and gestures in religious rites: 'No nation under heaven either doth or ever did suffer public actions which are of weight ... to pass without some visible solemnity, the very strangeness whereof and differences from that which is common, doth cause popular eyes to observe and to mark the same.' Yet the liturgical revival that occurred at the opening of the new century was to end in the catastrophe of the Civil War. Ceremonial and images were then put aside in the Church of England until the nineteenth century when the Oxford Movement rediscovered its Catholic roots.

There is some indication of the unpopularity of these changes in the reign of Edward VI: bequests to churches during these years plummeted from 65 to 15 per cent of what they had been before the reforms. This highlights an important fact. All these changes and reforms were expensive, yet they coincided with a dramatic fall in income from bequests, through the dissolution of the chantries and the suppression of church ales. Whether they could afford it or not, churchwardens had to purchase a Holy Table, a parish chest, a pulpit, an English Bible, the Book of Homilies and Erasmus's *Paraphrases on the New Testament*, a commentary on the four Gospels. Altars and steps leading up to them had to be levelled and the whole church, scarred by what had been ripped out, had to be whitewashed and then inscribed with suitable biblical texts. All of this cost money. At Smarden in Kent, for example, a chalice was sold to pay for 'a cloth to hang before the rood-loft to deface the monuments [and] tabernacles that wer yn the same roode lofte, written with scriptur and the Kynges armes'. Similar problems arose across the country as parishes struggled to comply with what had been imposed on them.

The suppressed anger, resentment and anguish of those caught up in these changes must have been immense. All the things which they were asked to destroy, or which were taken away from them, had been part of their daily lives for as long as anyone could remember. Many had deep personal meanings. Little wonder that it is precisely at this time that churchwardens began to sell things off rather than wait for them to be taken by government officials. Some were just spirited away into hiding in case events took a different direction.

*   *   *

The new religion. In the foreground, the ministry of the Word. Above, the two sacraments: the Lord's Supper and baptism.

And this is precisely what happened. The reforming king, the new Josiah who had felled the idols, died in 1553 and was succeeded by his sister Mary. She was the daughter of Henry VIII's first queen who had been sacrificed so that he could marry Anne Boleyn. And she, like her mother, was devoutly Catholic, so that now everything had to be set into reverse. In the countryside the return to the old Latin Mass was immediate and spontaneous; Protestantism in the main resided in the cities and towns. But it is of course always far easier to demolish something than to put it back; suddenly parishes were asked to restore their churches in a manner which had taken hundreds of years to accomplish. Yet the visitations were as demanding as their reforming predecessors and once again the process was expensive. The visitors were obsessed with checking that each church had a holy-water stoop and sprinkler, censers, processional crosses, a pax and a variety of other items for the performance of the Mass and the other great ceremonies. Just as the Edwardian visitors were intent on wiping out ceremonial so their Marian successors saw the key to their success in putting all of it back because from 'the observation of ceremonyes begynne the verye education of the chylderne of God'.

Head of Christ from a Rood, probably concealed at the Reformation in the nave of All Hallows, South Cerney, Gloucestershire.

We can trace what happened on the ground in the diocese of Gloucester where Bishop Hooper was promptly removed and later suffered a martyr's death at the stake. The Injunctions of 1556 began with bidding parishioners to go once more to church: 'there to hear Divine service, not in jangling or talking or walking commonly up and down, especially at mass time, but occupying themselves, according to the time and place, in godly meditation and prayer, either with beads or books of prayer allowed and appointed'. We get an indication that there had been a fall in church attendance during the reign of Edward, and it appears that those who did go didn't like what they saw. The Marian injunctions go on to prescribe that those present at Mass 'reverently kneel in such places of the church where they may both see and worship the Blessed Sacrament'. The clergy were to reinstate 'all godly ceremonies of the Church, as holy bread, holy water, bearing of palms, creeping to the cross, standing at the Gospel, [and] going on procession'. New choirs were to be formed and a tabernacle built for the Sacrament.

The response in the parishes was remarkably quick judging by the evidence of the 134 churchwardens' accounts that have survived. All of these churches had a High Altar by 1554, and by 1558, the year of Queen Mary's death, most had a Rood as well as a side altar, lights, statues, banners and other artefacts. Some items came out of hiding and were returned, others were bequeathed, and the rest came as the result of a parish levy. But by this time people were deeply mistrustful and wary. Thomas Morritt of Sherburn, Yorkshire, donated a collection of copes and vestments under the condition that if at any time they were about to be confiscated by the Crown, 'as of late tyme haythe ben', they were to be returned to his heirs. What the documents indicate is that the previous destruction had taken an appalling toll, particularly in parishes where the means were slender. A great deal now had to be improvised and done on the cheap. Ludham in Norfolk provides just one instance where the carved figures of Christ on the cross, Mary and John could not be afforded and so a painted canvas filled the space.

The make-shift painted Rood put up in Mary's short reign at St Catherine, Ludham, Norfolk.

* * *

One set of churchwardens' accounts provides a more amplified story, which has been told by the historian Eamon Duffy. Morebath was a remote Devonshire parish with a population of some 150 souls. Their priest for half a century was Sir Christopher Trychay and thanks to his accounts we get a rare glimpse of how the events I have described impinged on a small group of people. In 1520, when Trychay took over the parish, the church was filled with images, all of which had lights burning before them paid for by funds raised by various groups of villagers. Of the fifty-five taxpayers about thirty held some kind of office connected with the church. Trychay had a clerk to assist him in the performance of the liturgy saying or singing the responses, reading the Gospel, laying out the vestments and other liturgical artefacts, and distributing the holy bread and water.

The Act of Supremacy, which ended papal jurisdiction in 1534, hardly affected the good people of Morebath until the Act of Convocation abolished a tranche of holy days two years later. In Devon this meant the end of traditional religious feasts which had served as occasions for fairs and markets crucial to the local economy. This went hand in hand with the attack on images as superstition. Heads of households were now bidden to teach their servants the Lord's Prayer, the Ten Commandments and the Creed in English, and the Bible was to be read in both Latin and the vernacular. Reformers now gained positions of power within the area and the attack on traditional religion began in earnest. It was to be Thomas Cromwell's second set of injunctions, in 1538, which hit Morebath. The Great Bible in English had to be purchased, ornaments were removed from images and a book acquired to act as the parish register. Inevitably the various groups maintaining the votive lights dissolved and, as a consequence, the number of those directly involved with the church sank from twelve to six. Church ales were still produced but there was a sense of the parish drawing in on itself.

Still, when the evangelical Edward VI came to the throne in 1547,

The canvas at Ludham reversed and used to display the arms of Elizabeth I.

not that much had changed. Indeed, in that year the church had at last been able to buy the black vestments requisite for requiems. They had saved for these for a decade, yet within five years they were to be rendered redundant. The Injunctions of 1547 came like a bolt ordering the destruction of images and, later that year, the abolition of all chantries, which were billed as seats of 'blindness and ignorance'. At Morebath the church sheep were sold, further contributing to a severe financial crisis. Then the commissioners arrived with more demands: no cleric was to wear a black cape 'because it is thought to be a kind of monkery'; the solemn tolling of the church bells at funerals and on All Saints Day was forbidden; and, fatal for the church finances, church ales were banned 'because it hath been declare[d] unto us that many inconveniences hath come by them'. The churchwardens were expected to compensate for this shortfall in funds by an annual collection from the parish.

The services too began to change as the Prayer Book was introduced. Although Duffy in his story of this parish refers to the 'voices of Morebath', it is striking that, in fact, we hear no voices, apart from that of the priest; all we can do is read between the lines. At Morebath the destruction of images was a slow process but by Michaelmas 1548 most of them had gone. The Lent cloth which concealed the altar was sold, and so too were the hangings for the Easter Sepulchre, altar frontals, the veil which concealed the cross, streamers, banners, candlesticks and basins for tapers. Selling off items of this kind paid for the changes imposed by the state but with their passing went a whole world of memory and association.

The commissioners had asked for a complete inventory of the church's contents and assets. It was delivered to them in the spring of 1549 when, in response to their directives, a copy of Erasmus's *Paraphrases on the New Testament* was purchased for £1 on the security of Morebath's best crimson-velvet cope. To meet the bill everything from the church house which could be disposed of was sold: tables, planks, spits, a fireplace and a cupboard together with dishes of treen and pewter. By the close of 1549 Morebath had been rendered bankrupt, the church gutted, its ornaments destroyed, defaced or confiscated, and its corporate life dissolved. A decade earlier the parish under the aegis of its twelve officers – which had also included women – had an annual income of £10. Now there was just one warden left and a balance in hand of two shillings.

When unrest over enclosures and the introduction of the first Prayer Book in 1549 triggered off rebellion in the South-west, Morebath too sent its young men. One can guess their fate. Morebath bowed to the inevitable and in 1552 dismantled its altar, although Trychay continued to refer to the Holy Table as the altar. We know nothing of Morebath's reaction to the second Prayer Book but soon afterwards we witness the parish coping with the reversal of reforms under Catholic Mary. The progress was slow but the High Altar returned along with the Easter Sepulchre, the Sacrament in its pyx and a makeshift crucifix above the Rood. And then, suddenly, once more the tide changed when, on 17 November 1558, the queen's sister, Elizabeth, came to the throne. With her accession the story of the Reformation in England was to take a definite and sustained direction.

Chapter 4

Silence and Ambiguity

ST ISSUI'S CHURCH AT PARTRISHOW lies in the border country between Herefordshire and Wales. The drive to reach it is, at times, almost vertical and the sense of remoteness almost tangible. This is a church built on a steep eminence, the land falling sharply away on the south side from which the view is upwards across to the snow-capped Black Mountains and downwards towards a verdant valley. St Issui is visible evidence that the Reformation came slowly and reluctantly to such fastnesses. One senses that no one here in 1558 was in any hurry to embrace yet another swing of the theological pendulum. This, along with other areas, such as Lancashire, was a conservative and Catholic region.

Even after four hundred years the church's interior retains that sense of hesitancy, of a desire to hang on to things because nobody knows whether the pendulum might swing back yet again. So the delicately carved fifteenth-century screen remains intact, complete with its staircase access. The Rood figures of the crucified Christ flanked by Mary and John have gone but, below, on either side of the arch leading to the chancel, the visitor is startled to find two medieval stone altars with their consecration crosses untouched; their survival is almost unique. To the right, in front of one altar, stands a simple pulpit, not even elevated but just an enclosure for the minister to occupy. Here we see a juxtaposition of the old and the new, the sacrament-based and the Word-led religion. It looks as though those in control of St Issui were hedging their bets when Elizabeth came to the throne in 1558: it would have been easy to restore the church for pre-Reformation usage.

The rest of the building, however, is evidence that this never happened, for on the walls we see the prescribed texts: on the south wall the Ten Commandments, on the north the Creed, to which the royal arms were added later. Close by we read an inscription that sums up the history of the English parish church during those turbulent years: 'Let every soul subiect himself vnto the powers from high.' On the floor, against the wall, rests the parish chest carved from the solid trunk of a single tree. In that, responding to government directives, would have been locked away the parish registers.

No one could have predicted that the new queen would reign for forty-five years; her sister had governed the country for just six. There was indeed every possibility that things could have gone in reverse. When

St Issui, Partrishow, just a few miles over the Herefordshire border in Wales.

Elizabeth nearly died of smallpox at the close of the 1560s, her heir would have been the Catholic queen of Scots. Most of her major suitors were Catholic and if she had married, some accommodation would have been reached. And what would have happened if the Spanish Armada had made a successful invasion of England in 1588? In 1559 we witness the fourth change to religion in twenty years: it is hardly surprising that one senses people becoming more cautious and equivocal.

At the centre of the new reign was the so-called Elizabethan Settlement, which arrived as the Act of Uniformity in the spring of 1559, followed by a series of royal injunctions. Elizabeth had been inclined to reinstate the 1549 Prayer Book, but under pressure from the Protestant exiles returning from the continent, the act brought back that of 1552, albeit with slight modifications at the behest of the queen. The 1549 Prayer Book had been compiled under the aegis of Henry VIII's Archbishop of Canterbury, Thomas Cranmer. It was an attempt to give English Protestants an English-language service cleared of superstition. The Holy Communion was in English and retained the consecration of the elements but omitted the elevation of the Host and any suggestion of sacrifice. The laity were to receive both bread and wine. The doctrine of transubstantiation was replaced with a broader concept of the Real Presence of Christ, which nevertheless held that the body and blood of Christ are *actually* – not just figuratively or symbolically – received in the Sacrament. A cope could be worn for the Mass, and prayers for the dead were retained. The 1552 Prayer Book went much further. All references to the Mass and the altar were expunged, and vestments were reduced to a surplice only. Nearly all ceremonies were abolished and the baptism, confirmation and burial services rewritten. The Mass became a service of Holy Communion at a table, ordinary bread was to be used and placed in the hands, not the mouth, of the communicants. Where the new Prayer Book stood on eucharistic doctrine was not entirely clear but a shift towards the figurative and commemorative was clear.

Now, in 1559, the pendulum swung back again and the 1552 Book was modified, deleting the abusive reference to the pope in the Litany, reinstating vestments and introducing words at the delivery of Holy Communion which could be understood as confirming a more Catholic understanding of the Real Presence of Christ. The Royal Injunctions tried to back-pedal a little further, allowing, for example, the use of wafers as against the common white bread laid down for communion in the 1552 Prayer Book. Yet enough was left unspecified for the emerging Anglican Church to move in either a more Protestant or a more Catholic direction: here these ambiguities were etched in its future history. In the case of the Eucharist the injunctions could be read either as a vindication of the Real Presence or that the sacrament was a purely commemorative action. They could therefore be interpreted as calling for the return of altar, ceremonial and reverence at a great mystery presided over by a priest with supernatural powers; they could equally lead to a minister overseeing a meal of ordinary bread and wine distributed to the congregation assembled around a table. The queen had wanted to return to the Prayer Book of 1549 but the injunctions were carried out by the reformers back from the capital of extreme Protestantism, Calvin's Geneva, and they saw to it that her wishes were not respected.

But even so, there remained signs regarded with alarm by those who wanted to wipe out any memory of Catholicism. Although vest-

Receiving Holy Communion, 1578.

ments never came back into common use until the Victorian period, wearing a surplice was made mandatory. So too was the use of the sign of the cross at baptism. Processions ceased except for that at Rogationtide, which was regarded as essential for marking parish boundaries and thanking God for the fruits of the earth. At the name of Jesus people were bidden to bow. In effect, these government directives spelled out the fundamentals of worship while any major doctrinal issues were dodged, allowing as a result a good deal of private religious opinion as long as it remained just that – private.

This ambiguity was also reflected in the queen's intervention to avert the suppression of music in church. In a carefully worded passage the injunctions of 1559 permitted non-liturgical music:

> And that there be a modest distinct song, so used in all parts
> of the common prayers in the church, that the same may be
> as plainly understood, as if it were read without singing,
> and yet nevertheless, for the comforting of such that delight
> in music, it may be permitted that in the beginning, or in
> the end of common prayers, either at morning or evening,
> there may be sung an hymn, or such like song, to the praise
> of Almighty God, in the best sort of melody and music that
> may be conveniently devised, having respect that the sentence
> of the hymn may be understood and perceived.

This secured the future of music in cathedrals and the greater churches. As we shall see, it was not to have major implications for the parish church until much later.

The queen recognised something that bitterly frustrated the evangelical reformers returning from exile: you can't change the minds and actions of ordinary people quickly. The Act of Uniformity aimed to standardise the service, but what actually happened across the country was to remain far from uniform, certainly during the first decade of

Artefacts used in the pre-Reformation liturgy trodden underfoot by the Love of God, 1578.

Idolatry, is Spirituall adultery.

Elizabeth's reign and, in some instances, way beyond that. Yet, as I have indicated, the early visitations to the parishes in 1559 and throughout the early 1560s were pretty ruthless. The commissioners were bent on destroying any artefact used in Catholic ritual, not only checking up on everything in the church but seeking out and confiscating any items in private hands. In the early years of the queen's reign, the stress was on eliminating precisely those things that had been restored during the Marian revival of the 1550s. And this time they were burnt in the churchyard and on the village green.

But old habits die hard. In the diocese of Chester many rood-lofts still stood and others, although dismantled, 'lieth still ... ready to set up again'. Wafer bread was used well into the 1580s, and even as late as 1576 a cope was worn for Holy Communion at Compton Abdale in Gloucestershire. As the vast majority of priests remained in post, many external Catholic rituals must have continued within the framework of the Prayer Book service, which no visitation could wipe out. On Good Friday, the bishops bewailed, 'some certeyn persons go barefooted and barelegged to the churche, to creepe to the crosse'. During the new English service men and women in the pews continued to say the rosary or use their Latin primers – both now banned – just as they had during Mass. Some priests celebrated Holy Communion making it look as much like the banished Mass as possible, crossing and breathing on the elements which were elevated for adoration. Between 1563 and 1572 twenty-five priests were hauled up before the Ecclesiastical Commission at York and Chester for doing exactly this; yet all they received was an admonishment. As late as 1574 worshippers were still receiving the Sacrament in the mouth and not the hands, and holy water was still used as late as 1578 at St Helen's in Lancashire. In the same county the rood-loft at Stalmine was only dismantled in 1590. A group of ministers was to complain in the same year about those churchgoers who would continue to pray 'with crossing and knocking of their breast, and sometimes with beads closely handled'.

What the reformers celebrated as the conversion of England was to be a long haul and the means of coercing congregations were limited. Although fines were now introduced for those who failed to attend service, much depended on the local powers-that-be, government officers and landowners. Then there was the consistory court, the visitation process and the Ecclesiastical Commission. How far they went depended on their members; if conservatives predominated, a blind eye would be turned to the continuance of Catholic practices. For a large tract of the reign of Elizabeth the silent majority can be described as 'church papists', a term that first emerged in the 1580s. In 1596 a Carthusian monk, Thomas Cartwright, thought that most people were

The new religion of the Word.

'demi-catholickes, or catholique-like protestantes, or externall protestantes, and internall catholickes'.

Dr Alban Langdale, the former Marian archdeacon of Chichester,
deprived under Elizabeth, wrote in 1580: 'many parishes in England ther
be where neither the curate nor the parishioners are open professors of
Protestantism nor knowen Protestants but dissemblinge Catholickes'.
Francis Trigge, rector of Welborn in Lincolnshire and an avid supporter
of the Reformation writing thirty years into the reign in 1589, berated
the 'weeping and bewailing of the simple sort, and especially of women.
Who, going into the churches and seeing the bare walls, and lacking
their golden images, their costly copes, their pleasant golden chalices,
their goodly streamers, they lament in themselves and fetch many deep
sighs, and bewail this spoiling and laying waste of the Church . . .'. Even
the Canons of 1604, by which time the Anglican Church was defining

The Protestant view of the old religion.

its theological position sharply vis-à-vis both Catholics and Puritans, recognised that the Church of England was made up of 'popishly given' people. This went on well into the Stuart period; John Earle in his *Microcosmography* (1628) paints a vivid picture of a 'church papist' slumped in his pew, 'his hat over his eyes'.

Even after the queen was excommunicated by Pope Pius V in 1570 there was still no real pressure on those known to be Catholic to attend church, although the legal structure to enforce compliance was already in place: the Act of Uniformity of 1559 imposed a fine of twelve pence for non-attendance. What the state demanded was outward conformity; it didn't enquire into people's private consciences. During the first decade of Elizabeth's rule, little or no pressure was exerted and, in any case, there were many ways of avoidance. Coming late was one, bribing the parson or the churchwardens another. There also emerged the custom of occasional conformity by the head of the household. Later, when the

Crown began addressing the issue of flagrant non-attendance or re-
cusancy, those who defied the new faith and obeyed the papal instruction
never to go to the heretical services, turned out to be a small and prosperous group able to cope with the heavy fines imposed. For poor
Catholics there was no alternative but to attend the Protestant parish
church unless they found service and protection in a well-to-do Catholic
household. In response to Catholic plots against the queen and the war
with Catholic Spain, Catholicism was progressively cast as being un-
patriotic and, from 1581 onwards, statutes that introduced crippling fines
were passed by a Parliament dominated by Protestants of Puritan persuasion. But this opting-out of parishioners resulted in the first break-up
of the English parish as a cohesive social unit.

The recusants remained outside the church. Far more disruptive and
dangerous were those at the opposite end of the theological spectrum.
The Puritans were dissatisfied with the settlement of 1559 and bent on
destroying 'the dregs of popery' in the Church's rituals. They were a
group of literate and often highly articulate people acting like a fifth
column to undermine and radically change the Church of England
through sympathisers and activists in Parliament. Some aimed to reform
the Church of England from within by peaceful means; others wanted
England to turn Calvinist and join their co-religionists on the European
mainland. In that they were to fail, but up and down the country, and
more particularly in the towns, the Puritans were to take over parish
life. The absence of precise instructions was to allow the godly, as those
Puritans were called, to perform the services of the Book of Common
Prayer in a far more reformist way than was ever intended, in particular with a strong emphasis on the sermon. The Anglican position was
that reading the Scriptures was a sermon in itself but to the godly this
was insufficient: Scripture called for exposition and commentary from
the pulpit. The godly equally disliked the Anglican insistence on corporate prayer demanding instead extempore ejaculation, an outpouring of

the Holy Spirit. Finally, to them the church was not a sacred space: the true Church was not a building but the godly themselves.

It is difficult for many today to grasp the attraction of a radical belief in justification by faith alone: that human beings are lifted from sin and redeemed by God without any merit or religious 'work'. The Puritans firmly believed that the godly were the chosen ones, God's 'elect' from the world's creation. Everyone else was excluded and, therefore, damned. Where the godly got a foothold in a parish, they would often tear it apart. They disrupted erstwhile peaceful communities with what they preached and their efforts to discipline those they regarded as godless. Villages could be factionalised as sinners were denounced, resulting in a flood of court cases and bitter divisions within the parish, and soon the godly started suppressing the sports traditional after church on a Sunday in order to establish the biblical observance of the Sabbath.

By the middle of Elizabeth's reign the godly had formed a church within the Church. Puritan parishes would come together in groups of twelve known as a *classis*; delegates from twenty-four of these made up a synod. Only by the 1590s did the Established Church gather the strength to suppress them, a process that reached its culmination in the Canons of 1604, the first occasion on which the Church of England spelled out its disciplinary position in any detail. The next century would show whether the godly could be contained within the fledgling Church of England or whether, like the recusant Catholics, they too would leave.

In the picture I have sketched so far, religious practice in Elizabethan England emerges as a pretty piecemeal affair. Yet we lack evidence of what ordinary people thought of it all. Here, again, Eamon Duffy's account of what happened in Morebath makes fascinating reading. The parish had, of course, welcomed the Marian revival, brought back the High Altar and reinstated the Easter Sepulchre. Vestments came out of hiding and were returned. When all this was again reversed the response was far more cautious. In 1559 any items required for Catholic ritual were given to various parish members for safekeeping, a vivid demonstration of a hedging of theological bets. In that year altars were demolished and a copy of the new Book of Common Prayer purchased. In 1561 tablets inscribed with the Ten Commandments, the Creed and the Lord's Prayer were put up over the communion table, and the year after the rood-loft was dismantled. But it was not until 1571 that the parish purchased Erasmus's *Paraphrases*, the second volume of homilies and a copy of the Thirty-Nine Articles, which defined the doctrinal position of the Church of England and had been issued by the Convocation, the governing body of the Church, in 1563. Two years later they acquired Bishop Jewel's *Apology*, the classical defence of the Anglican Church.

Morebath reveals a slow and gradual process of religious transformation. Like every other parish, the congregation had put the clock back willingly under Queen Mary, and the old sense of community had returned with the parishioners working together to provide all the items required for the restoration of the old liturgy. And then, suddenly, it all went into reverse yet again. But the Elizabethan Settlement brought none of the violence of the Edwardian era. The priest, Sir Christopher Trychay, remained with his flock, still Catholic at heart but going along with it all. He continued to call the Holy Table an altar and over it draped a carpet made from banned vestments. Before the Reformation, many within the village community had been involved in the church, raising money and taking part in various ceremonies. Processions, lighting candles before the Rood and images, and prayers for the dead had drawn the community together. But all of that had disappeared. Now it was the churchwardens who were responsible for poor relief, the repair of the roads and bridges, and, of course, the church fabric. They recorded church attendance and closely watched the cleric to make sure that he kept to the Book of Common Prayer. The church and its officers had become an arm of the state.

All this caused an enormous disruption of parish life. Bequests and benefactions naturally plummeted, not only because such acts no longer aided salvation but also because the state was seen to be predatory: what was given voluntarily one year could easily be carted away by government officials the next. Fortunately some fund-raising activities, such as the sale of church ales, revived under Mary, continued; otherwise the church would have sunk into insolvency. By the close of Elizabeth's reign the parishioners of Morebath were able to raise as much as £50–60 a year towards maintaining church and churchyard. In spite of all the changes it seems that enough religious life was left to ensure some kind of continuity.

I have postponed any discussion of the services of the Book of Common Prayer until this point because it wasn't until after the defeat of the Spanish Armada in 1588 that it became firmly established: after the queen's victory over Catholic Spain it was clear to everyone that it was here to stay. Compiled by a committee of reformist theologians, the Prayer Book of 1552 – revised and reissued in 1559 – had been edited by Thomas Cranmer, and it was his genius that created a work that was to frame the English mind and language, together with its spiritual sensibilities, for the next four centuries. According to Eamon Duffy, for the average congregation, 'Cranmer's sombrely magnificent prose, read week by week, entered and possessed their minds and became the fabric of their prayer, the utterance of their most solemn and vulnerable moments.' It could never have made such an impact without the aid of the printing press, nor without Cranmer's quite exceptional rhythm of prose and nobility of style. The incantatory power of his prayers is reflected in the fact that so many are retained, albeit revised, in the current services of the worldwide Anglican Communion.

The Book of Common Prayer was unlike anything produced by the Reformation in continental Europe. Its central aim was to enable ordinary people to take full part in worship, and in order to achieve it Cranmer composed a dramatic ceremonial to be performed by the entire

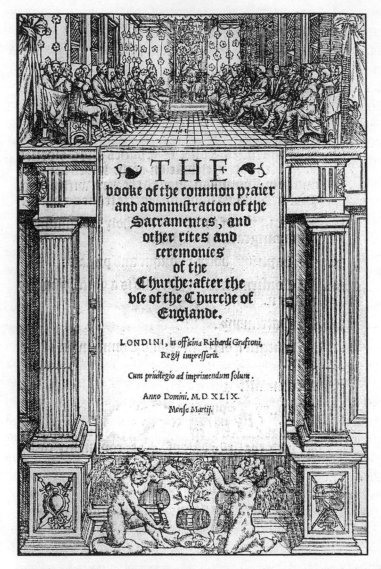

The Book of Common Prayer, 1549.

community day by day, week by week. 'From henceforth all the whole Realm shall have but one Use,' proclaimed the 1549 version in a statement that was equally applicable to the Prayer Books of 1552 and 1559. The first Prayer Book abolished the medieval liturgy lock, stock and barrel but still referred to Mass and altar and retained the use of vestments. The recitation of the bede-roll disappeared, and the congregation was to receive communion in both kinds. The 1552 version was far more radical, the Mass becoming Holy Communion and the altar the Holy Table. The services were carefully compiled to articulate the role of the worshipper and thereby demonstrate the essential unity of the whole Christian community. The use of the word 'common' in its title emphasised that the book contained prayers to be used by the whole community, which they were to recite together and eventually learn by heart. Thus the book set out to dissolve the old belief that saw the priest as being set apart by emphasising instead the equality of the minister with his lay congregation.

The Prayer Book taught the belief in justification by faith alone and that salvation could never be obtained through good works. But justification by faith in the Anglican sense was never as exclusive as in its interpretation by the Puritans. Salvation and justification were determined by God's eternal decree of election but – and this was where the Anglican theologians parted company with the godly – the elect were known only to God. As a consequence no one should be excluded from the services and sacraments of the Church. Moreover, justification came through 'hearing the Word of God'. It is important to remember that the majority of any Elizabethan country congregation would have been illiterate. This accounts for the many readings from Scripture during the service, which were arranged so 'that all the whole Bible (or the greatest parte thereof) should be read over in the year'. In this way the minister would 'be stirred up to godliness' and the congregation 'profite more and more'. This strong emphasis on Scripture readings would account for the fact that from the middle of

the 1570s the Prayer Book was often bound up with the Bible, physical evidence of their being seen as a unity.

Before the Reformation, the churchgoer had experienced the strict
separation of priest and congregation, both acting almost independently
of one another. The priest would be saying Mass and the congregation
would be at their separate prayers and beads, the two coming together
only at the adoration of the Host. This was now substituted by a service
that was based on the premise that communal public prayer had more
virtue, and that it was more important for the community to *act* together
in this way than to *listen* to a sermon. Here the Prayer Book distanced
itself from the godly to whom the exposition of the Word of God by
the minister in the pulpit took precedence over any other form of
communal worship.

*　*　*

A chancel remodelled for Holy Communion, Hailes, Gloucestershire, early
seventeenth century.

Not everything, however, went as initially planned. It appears that the weekly communion as envisioned by Thomas Cranmer and the other reformers never became commonplace. Their intention had been that the congregation would assemble every Sunday for matins, leading on to the celebration of communion, followed by the sermon. Yet this sequence fell by the wayside almost at the outset and didn't become the norm in the Church of England until the middle of the twentieth century. One reason was the expense of communion in terms of bread and wine for what could be a large number of parishioners who had to attend, as it was laid down in the 1559 Act of Uniformity. The Prayer Book itself stipulated communion three times a year as the minimum, at Christmas, Easter and, perhaps, Palm Sunday. But that aspiration was abandoned in the Canons of 1571, which specified that only communion at Easter was obligatory. It is ironic that despite Cranmer's intentions the pre-Reformation practice of annual communion re-emerged so quickly. But even the administration of communion once a year presented some parishes with enormous problems. At Allerton in Northumberland as many as 600 needed to be given their Easter communion, which meant that a series of services had to be held. Here it was recorded that the 'great number doe make such a confusion and noise and thronging that oftentimes the young and old people are carried downe with their crouding'.

Communion was held in high esteem in early modern England. It was an event for which the churchgoer dressed in his best clothes, and there was a considerable flurry of devotional literature whereby the communicant could prepare himself. One aspect of the sacrament in particular became firmly rooted in popular culture: its role as a reconciling force within the community. The Book of Common Prayer excluded from communion anyone living in 'open and notorious evil' or any persons 'betwixt whom he [i.e. the minister] perceiveth malice and hatred to reign'. Communicants had to be in charity in order to receive the sacrament and records show that many therefore forfeited the rite. Recusants, of course, welcomed this as a means whereby to avoid contamination with heresy. Yet others set about peacemaking before the event. But where the godly prevailed we learn of instances when ministers denied the sacrament to parishioners they regarded unfit to receive it.

Communion was of course also a means of reinforcing social distinction. It was administered strictly according to rank, first to aristocracy and gentry and then, gradually, down the line. In some parishes in Elizabethan times there were even two kinds of communion wine in use, with a better one, such as muscadine, for the higher ranks of the community.

With communion reduced to an annual event, the service was enacted each Sunday in somewhat truncated form, which became nevertheless the norm right into the twentieth century. Ralph Holinshed, the first edition of whose *Chronicles* appeared in 1577 – a quarry used by Shakespeare for his history plays – gives a rare contemporary account of churchgoing in the middle of Elizabeth's reign:

> After a certain number of psalms read, which [are] limited according to the dates of the month, for morning and evening prayer, we have two lessons, whereof the first is taken out of the old testament, the second out of the new . . . After morning prayer we have the litany and suffrages . . . This being done, we proceed unto the communion, if any communicants be to receive the eucharist: if not we read the Decalogue, epistle and gospel, with the Nicene creed (of some in derision called the dry communion), and then proceed unto an homily or sermon, which hath a psalm before and after it, and finally unto the baptism of such infants as on every Sabbath day (if occasion require) are brought unto the churches; and thus is the forenoon bestowed. In the afternoon likewise we meet again, and after psalms and lessons ended, we have commonly

Baptism, 1578.

a sermon, or at leastwise our youth catechised by the space
of an hour. And thus do we spend the Sabbath day in good
and godly exercises, all done in the vulgar tongue, that each
one present may hear and understand the same.

Without a sermon this ceremony lasted about an hour; with a sermon
it could last two hours and, in the case of the godly, considerably
longer.

Did music continue to have a place in the parish church? The
dissolution of the chantries ended the careers of a large number of
professional musicians. Where there had been a tradition of sung
services, it was now reduced to the clerk and the few singers he could
muster from among the congregation. The service in the vernacular
rendered the settings for the Latin Mass obsolete, and there was an
attempt during the Edwardian period to reset the new service, mainly
by adapting music from the old rite. John Marbecke's *Booke of common
praier noted* (1550) tried this, partly by adapting plainsong, partly by
incorporating original melody in a similar style. But after 1559 sung
services in the parish church were abandoned, altogether. Organs
were initially kept going but between 1570 and 1585 they too were

abandoned, not to return until the Victorian period. They were replaced with the congregational singing of metrical psalms, a practice that had been brought back from the continent by Protestant exiles. It soon caught on and became immensely popular – although it was disliked by both the queen and the aristocratic and gentry classes as 'smacking too much of Geneva'. There was no mention in the 1559 Prayer Book that psalms could be sung but it happened nonetheless. Thomas Sternhold and John Hopkins's *The whole booke of psalms* (1562) was to go through 600 editions over the next 125 years. Although Sternhold's verse left much to be desired, its language was direct and simple and the metre he employed uniform.

The Elizabethan Church was haunted by its lack of a preaching ministry for most of the reign. The 1559 injunctions laid down that every parish should listen to at least one sermon every month, either by the incumbent, if he had a licence, or by someone who held one. Yet a year later the hoped-for monthly sermon had become a quarterly event. It was not until the Jacobean period that the sermon became a regular part of the service: any visitor to a country church will usually find the pulpit dating from that time. Almost thirty years into the queen's reign only a fifth of the incumbents had a licence, and in 1584 it was calculated that only 600 of the country's 9,000 parishes yielded enough income to support a cleric educated enough to preach.

Congregations were not allowed to go uninstructed, however, and in the absence of a sermon, one of the homilies was to be read to them. There were two books of homilies, the first prepared in the reign of Henry VIII but not issued until after the accession of his son in 1547. This was an initial selection of twelve, several the work of Thomas Cranmer, covering subjects not only concerned with doctrine, like 'A fruitful Exhortation to the Reading of Holy Scripture' or 'Of the true and lively Faith', but also with morals, such as 'Against Swearing and Perjury' and, a subject dear to Tudor government, 'An Exhortation to Obedience'. In 1571 a second book containing another twenty-one homilies was issued, this time in the main composed by Bishop John Jewel, the leading Anglican theologian.

This too confirms that there was no overnight transformation of the country, and in that sense the Reformation imposed from on high has to be regarded a failure. As late as 1597 eighty-eight churches in Norfolk still failed to have even a quarterly sermon and in seventeen even homilies weren't read. But the Book of Common Prayer gradually left its imprint. Memories of the old rituals of the past began to fade, and in the case of the young, mandatory attendance every second Sunday and holy day before evensong for at least half an hour's instruction in the catechism ensured that they at least knew that. Catechism was extended in 1571 to include servants and to take place every Sunday. No one was to receive communion until they knew the Lord's Prayer, the Ten Commandments and the Creed by heart.

The catechism contained in the Prayer Book was brief. A second catechism, compiled by Alexander Nowell, Dean of St Paul's, was published in 1570 but it ran to 176 pages and was therefore too long. The result was a steady stream from the presses of thirty- to forty-page alternatives aimed at 'the ruder sort', 'the meaner sort', 'the common sort', or the 'common people'. These inculcated the need for rigorous self-examination before Holy Communion and the necessity for a general understanding

Catechising, 1578.

of its significance, thus providing the minimum standard of religious knowledge required of any parishioner.

What was it like to go to a country church in Elizabeth's reign? We need to start with the building itself, which remained a potent symbol of continuity through all the convulsions. After the Marian interval, the Advertisements of 1566, compiled by Elizabeth's Archbishop of Canterbury, Matthew Parker, not only laid down practices such as kneeling to receive communion and the sign of the cross at baptism, but also dictated the internal arrangements of churches. The images and altars had gone, and the walls were once again whitewashed and adorned with biblical texts. The font was still where it always had been, as was the screen dividing nave from chancel, but both Rood and loft went. In the chancel, usually against the east wall, stood the Holy Table covered with a cloth, the Ten Commandments suspended above it. It was only brought forward into the chancel when communion was celebrated, a 'fair linen cloth' cast over it for the occasion. In parishes that were Puritan strongholds the table would stand there the whole time, surrounded by seating. Over the screen, and replacing the Rood, there would be displayed the royal arms. In the main body of the nave, just to one side of the opening in the screen, stood the pulpit, the place from which the minister led the congregation.

The Elizabethan Book of Homilies included one 'for repairing and keeping clean, and comely adorning of churches'. This enunciated to the congregation an agenda of good housekeeping but, more significantly, redefined the nature of the church building. It opened by explaining that the church was a building 'that God may have his place, and that God may have his time, duly to be honoured and served of the multitude in the Parish'. To it the parish should resort to hear God's words and know his will, to receive the sacraments, and here, together, the 'whole multitude of God's people in the Parish' should pray, give thanks to God and bestow alms. Like any dwelling house it should maintain 'all things in good order, and all corners clean and sweet'. There should be 'places convenient to sit on', a pulpit and the Lord's Table for 'his holy supper' and a font for baptism.

William Harrison, in his *Description of England* (1575), is another contemporary who paints a vivid picture of the Elizabethan Sunday and its physical setting:

> ... whereas there was wont to be a great partition between the choir and the body of the church, now it is either very small or none at all, and, to say the truth, altogether need-less, sith the minister saieth his service commonly in the body of the church with his face toward the people, in a little taber-nacle of wainscot provided for the purpose; by which means the ignorant do not only learn divers of the Psalms and usual prayers by heart, but also such as can read do pray together with him, so that the whole congregation at one instant pour out their petitions unto the living God for the whole estate of His church in most earnest and fervent manner ...

Compared with the hurly-burly which had preceded it the atmos-phere must have been far more constrained. The sexes on the whole continued to be segregated, and seating, which now became common-place, continued to be fixed according to social status and habitation, with the lower classes and the young consigned to benches at the west end. Although the overall trend was towards the family pew – which arrived in the next century – on the whole there was a concern about men and women sitting together 'promiscuously'. Studies of local records show no uniform approach, although what was decided at Earls Colne in 1617 throws interesting light on the issue. Here it was stipulated that men and women should sit opposite each other, that those hard of hearing should be closer to the pulpit and that it was inappropriate for older women and church elders to sit lower than maids and young women, 'who bore no charge about the mainteynance of the church'.

All over England in the late Elizabethan and early Jacobean periods churchwardens were busy allocating seats according to 'ranks', 'qualities' and 'degrees', often resulting in ferocious disputes in the courts. When the gentry entered the congregation stood up. In this way the post-Reformation parish church continued to define community in terms of hierarchy. In 1635, the Temple family in Stowe in Buckinghamshire asked the vicar and churchwardens to place the parishioners 'according to their degree and quality'. They complained that at present 'most of the parishioners do place theselves unreverently and without any order, some young men and servants taking place of married men and some maids sitting above married women, not having any respect unto the quality and conditions of the person at all'.

On Sundays everyone in the parish – or so it was laid down – had to attend church both in the morning and afternoon. The Sunday service was where rich and poor, high and low, young and old corporately gathered: they sat down together, spoke and sang the same words, and went through the same rituals. While in the medieval period pews were only for the wealthy, in the new dispensation everyone was accorded a seat. The church would have been crowded and with no heating it must have been freezing cold in winter. In summer the problem was somewhat different, for the heat would make the stench of the bodies almost unbearable. There could also be angry scenes as people jostled for seating if they thought that their position in the social hierarchy had been usurped. At Wing in Berkshire, for example, Alice Maynard was had up 'for thrusting Anne Parratt up and downe a seate ... and for pulling of her hat from her head, and throwing it into the end of the other seate ...'

It would be wrong to assume that Elizabethan congregations were all quiescent. They could spit, tell jokes, knit or humiliate the preacher with taunts and jibes during the sermon. When the curate of Storgursey in Somerset went on too long, a member of the congregation bellowed out that it was time for him to come out of the pulpit so that the maids might go milking. A Cambridgeshire man in 1598 was charged for indecent behaviour in church, for his 'most loathsome farting, striking and scoffing speeches'. Nor should we forget that not everyone went to church: the application of mandatory attendance did not extend to those at the bottom of the social ladder. But even those who did attend would have had only superficial knowledge of the faith. The medieval church had never set out to burden the parishioner with theological detail but to engage him in corporate ritual. After the Reformation the appalling ignorance of the majority of the congregation was first blamed on popery and then on the lack of instruction from godly preachers before the clergy were forced to accept that ignorance was the norm with which they had to live.

Occasionally the proceedings in church were enlivened by an act of public penance, yet only in the case of extreme offences was this performed in the presence of the entire congregation at Morning Prayer. For minor offences, like absence from church, or working on Sundays and holy days, it was enough to appear before the minister and the churchwardens. Drunkenness, holding conventicles – illegal religious meetings in private houses – or, in the case of a churchwarden, failing in the job, called for confession not only before minister and church-wardens but also a select group of parishioners. Finally, there was public penance visited on those who had sexual relations outside marriage. The offender had to parade bareheaded, barelegged and barefooted, robed in a white sheet and bearing a white wand, to the church and stand 'in the sight of the congregation till the gospel is to be read and then standing upon a step or two high near the ministers deske the better to be heard and seene of the congregation' admitting that they had 'committed the vile ands heinous sinne of ffornication'.

Everybody must have noticed the appalling state of repair into which many churches began to fall, and that church building had stopped almost completely. Even the Puritan, Philip Stubbes, author of the *Anatomy of*

Abuses (1581), couldn't ignore the fact during a tour of England. Looking back he was forced to admit that earlier generations had left a mighty architectural legacy: 'And for good works, who seeth not that herein they went far beyond us ... What memorable and famous buildings, what stately edifices of sundry kinds ... What churches, Chapels and other houses of prayer did erect ...' Horrified by the state of the churches he visited, Stubbes recorded collapsed roofs with the rain flooding in, floors of sand and dust or, at best, covered only with grass or sedge, and pews in such a disgusting state 'as would make a man loth to come in them'. Centuries of pride in building, expanding and adorning churches had ground to a halt, not to be revived until the very close of Elizabeth's reign when the conditions Stubbes recorded demanded remedial action. If there was adornment of any kind it was the vulgar addition of aristocratic and gentry tombs, gaudily coloured, and often sited where altars had once stood. As we have seen, the invasion of church interiors by secular tombs had been well under way before the Reformation, but what made it so intrusive now was that these marbled tombs, gaudily bedizened with coats of arms, were the *only* recent additions to church interiors, turning them into Valhallas of the ruling establishment. No longer did inscriptions ask for the prayers of the living; instead the tombs celebrated the family connections and secular offices held by the deceased. Images of the establishment classes replaced the images of saints.

While in the past many groups had been involved in the maintenance of the church, its income was now gradually reduced to one source, the tithe. Consequently by 1600 the tithe was increasingly resented as the minister was viewed less as 'one of us', a working villager, than a man who lived off other people's labours, taking a percentage of all parishioners' produce, such as eggs, milk and fruit. The result was a growing distance between the cleric and his flock; the clergy had not yet become gentry but it had begun the trajectory. The cleric could also now be a married man, a change that would have taken time to be accepted.

The images of the ruling élite replacing those of the saints at St Mary the Virgin, Bottesford, Leicestershire.

The minister was assisted by the parish clerk, a man appointed by the incumbent. Edmund Grindal, archbishop of York from 1570 to 1575, defined his role. First and foremost he must obey the parson and then 'be able to read the first lesson, the epistle and the psalms, with answer to the suffrages as is used, and that he keep the books and ornaments of the church fair and clean . . . and also that he endeavour himself to teach young children to read if he be able to do so'. The Canons of 1603 also included as desirable a 'competent skill in singing (if it may be)'.

But perhaps the greatest shift was the transformation of the role of the parish officers: what had been an expression of parish democracy now became the prerogative of a few important families and an arm of the State. Henceforth the chief lay officers of the parish were to be the churchwardens, elected annually at Easter. Their task was to see that the church was equipped with the correct books, the Bible, the Book of Common Prayer, the homilies, Erasmus's *Paraphrases*, a calendar and, sometimes, John Foxe's Protestant martyrology, *Actes and Monuments*. The churchwardens had to purchase wine and bread for communion and see to it that the Holy Table was covered for the event with 'a faire linen clothe' or 'some coveringe of silke buckram or other such like'. They were also to check that the church was equipped with a communion cup (replacing the medieval chalice), a surplice, a pulpit, a register and two chests, one for alms and another for records. They had to keep watch that the church was not profaned by feasting and drinking and that the churchyard was kept tidy. They exerted power by policing community morals, reporting on a whole list of offenders, such as persistent drunkards and blasphemers, people who came late to church or not at all, those who failed to pay their church dues, those who married without the banns being read or within the bounds of affinity, and finally those who were 'favourers of the Romishe or forreyne power'.

Thus Church and State became coextensive in Elizabethan England: everyone had to be a member of the Church of England and Catholics

The church stripped bare, St Andrew, Westhall, Suffolk.

were excluded from office. The old liturgical year was gradually replaced with annual services in celebration of the State. The most important was that marking the queen's Accession Day, 17 November; in 1576 a special service was introduced for that occasion, and subsequent reigns were to add others.

The absence of Christ's presence in the pyx suspended above the altar with its lights below, the snuffing out of the flickering candles before the Rood and the destruction of an abundance of sculpted and painted imagery stripped church interiors of any sense of mystery or the supernatural. For those who lived through these decades it must have been agonising to stare at the empty niches where once a statue of the Virgin or saint had stood, contemplating the vast areas of whitewash, which now covered cycles depicting the Gospel story, not to mention looking up at the arms of the queen where once they had contemplated Christ crucified. Now the only decorations were inscriptions of the Ten Commandments, the Lord's Prayer and the Creed alongside biblical texts. These exhorted the congregation to obedience to the powers-that-be, spelled out the duties of a parent, a child, a husband or a wife. One is reminded of the Chinese Cultural Revolution: so much trauma visited on so many ordinary people and so little voice given to express what must have been an overwhelming sense of anguish and loss. Of course, we only know about the period through those who were literate and permitted to express what they felt. We can only guess at what went through the minds of those who had no voice as they sat in church on Sunday. Outward conformity, after all, was what government demanded. No one was ever asked to express a view about their beliefs or an opinion about the new services and rituals. The church thus ceased to be the lively centre of a community led by faith and became instead an arm of the State whose aim was obedience and submission.

What had been the major changes to the average parish church in the countryside by the time the queen died in 1603? Services in the vernacular were certainly new. Novel too was the strong focus on readings from Scripture and the hour-long sermon (when it happened). Psalm singing too had become hugely popular. The visual elements had been ruthlessly expunged; images, colour and spectacle vanished. A whole cycle of ceremonial was suppressed: the bearing of candles at Candlemas, the imposition of ashes on Ash Wednesday, the bearing of palms in procession on Palm Sunday, the rites of Maundy Thursday along with the Easter Sepulchre, creeping to the cross on Good Friday, and the bearing of the sacrament in cavalcade at Corpus Christi. No more was there holy water sprinkled on the congregation, the pax kissed or holy bread distributed.

But, and that is the paradox of it all, people still went to the same building every Sunday. Continuity was also sustained by the fact that most clergy stayed put and saw their congregations through every change. The parish church was still central to village life. It remained the centre of Christian society, and the means whereby ordinary people sought their

The creation of a new pantheon of Protestant martyrs.

spiritual identity. The sacraments – albeit reduced to two, baptism and Holy Communion – were still administered. And it was in church that people were baptised, married and buried. Yet in their zeal to wipe out purgatory and the whole body of Masses and prayers for the departed, the reformers had left little comfort to the bereaved. Nothing in this new faith was quite so brutal as the inability of the living even to pray for the dead.

In church people still sought forgiveness for their transgressions either through congregational confession or by seeking out the minister for personal guidance or absolution. The bells still rang and looking beyond the bounds of the parish, the old parochial structure was still in place. The Church of England remained Christocentric, its main holy days being those of Christmas, the Annunciation, Good Friday and Easter. A single procession also survived at Rogationtide, and several minor gestures and ceremonies continued, such as kneeling for communion, bowing at the name of Jesus and the sign of the cross at baptism.

By the close of Elizabeth's reign the services of the Book of Common Prayer were well on the way to substituting one traditional religion for another. Within two generations it was being referred to as 'the ancient order of the Church of England'. By that date too the might of Spain had been vanquished by a people who, thanks to a weekly intake of Scripture, equated themselves with God's chosen people. The victory over Spain was interpreted as a divine sign bestowed on the Anglican Church by God, one which had been sealed by the blood of martyrs described by Foxe. His *Actes and Monuments* inculcated into people a Protestant view of the country's history, one in which a nation had been enslaved by a corrupt papacy and rescued by an enlightened monarchy. In the people's imagination the medieval saints were replaced by those who had been burnt for heresy in the reign of Mary. And gradually the Book of Common Prayer became sanctified, so much so that by the next reign it could be extolled as 'not the like this day extant in Christendom'.

By that time the silent majority had come to terms with an ambiguous form of Protestantism that was unique in Western Europe. It was a faith that demanded only attendance and then left parishioners to think Christianly what they liked. This comfortable ambiguity was both its strength and its weakness, as indeed it is to this day. Although it was decidedly Protestant the few texts that defined the Church could manoeuvre it in both more Catholic as well as more sharply Protestant directions. By 1600 we sense a recognition of the Church's pre-Reformation inheritance as Anglican theologians began to elaborate on its role as the old medieval *Ecclesia Anglicana* purged and reformed. Was this a response to the fact that a swathe of residual Catholics still sat in the pews? The chances of the Church of England returning to Rome could be ruled out but, at least for the Elizabethan and Jacobean periods, those who emphasised its Catholic roots and traditions could be accommodated within its theological spectrum. In the coming century that accommodation was to break down as the Church of England constructed an identity that left no room for ambiguity and manoeuvre. The uniformity demanded by the Act of 1559 was imposed for the very first time on every parish church. The historian Diarmaid MacCulloch perceptively described what happened in England as 'the building of a Protestant Church which remained haunted by its Catholic past'. That past was to return forcefully in the new century.

Chapter 5

The Beauty of Holiness

THE DORE VALLEY IN HEREFORDSHIRE is of a surpassing beauty, one of those remote sites chosen by Cistercian monks in the middle of the twelfth century for a monastery. No visit leaves me unmoved by the tranquillity of this hidden spot held in by gently rolling hills and through which a tributary of the Wye runs. Today, what is left of the red sandstone abbey arises in truncated form, a shape it took in the early 1630s when what had been reduced to a ruin at the Dissolution was restored as a handsome parish church.

A visit to Abbey Dore is one of those rare magical experiences of stepping back into the past, for we enter a world that virtually vanished in the Civil War. Here survives intact that phase in the history of our parish churches known as 'the beauty of holiness'. As soon as one's feet touch the stone-flagged floor one is aware that the ethos is very different from that of the previous century. Scattered across the honey-coloured walls are figures and biblical texts framed in elaborate decorative cartouches. Close to the entrance comes the apposite: 'I had rather be a door keeper in the house of my God: than dwell in the tents of ungodliness.' Above a musician's gallery at the west end, we see the Old Testament king David, harp in hand, with the exhortation: 'Young men and maidens, old men and children, praise the name of the Lord.' Below that gallery, erected after the Civil War, there would have stretched the pews and, to one side, the pulpit.

Before them the congregation would have looked at the robust wood-work of the screen with its Latin inscription: 'Live in a pleasing way to God, buried to the evil of this world, ready to pass over to the next world.' But what lies beyond, as we step into the chancel area, would have been viewed by many with alarm, for here we find the old stone altar used by

St Mary, Abbey Dore, Herefordshire.

the monks restored to its place and fenced in by wooden rails, or balus-
ters, two features we now take for granted but at the time were revolutionary. To emphasise the altar's sanctity it has not only been fenced off
but the approach to it has steps. Even more surprising, as we lift our eyes
up to the great east window, is to find new stained glass in rich shades
of gold, ochre, blue and crimson peopled by saints and prophets attending
the Ascension of Christ. We are witnessing the return of images.

All this could easily have been read by those who worshipped here
as a return to Catholicism, for such an arrangement centred less on the
Word than on the Sacrament. This is the church building seen again as
sacred space, of the Protestant Holy Table recast as altar, which must
be venerated and protected from profanation, for upon it Christ is present
in the Eucharist. At Abbey Dore we find a strong sense of order and
decorum and an unashamed return to decoration and imagery that seems
a world away from the iconoclasm of the previous century. What we
witness here is the parish church rediscovered and reborn.

A slate plaque on the north wall, dating from 1739, tells us that

A great part of this CHURCH being broken down ... This
Remainder ... was restored to a Sacred Use, the *Walls* therof
being greatly repaired, the *Roof* and *Tower* entirely rebuilt,
the *Rectory* founded and very bountifully endow'd ... by the
Pious and ever memorable JOHN Lord Viscount SCUDA-
MORE upon 22d day of *March Anno Domini 1634.*

This inscription is amplified by the coats of arms on the chancel screen:
those of Lord Scudamore, of King Charles I, whom he served, and of
the archbishop of Canterbury, William Laud, the Viscount's great
friend and spiritual mentor.

Lord Scudamore was born in 1601, two years before the death of
Elizabeth I. He belonged to a generation that had no memory of Catholic
England; yet we see at Abbey Dore that he did not reject the Catholic
past. Indeed, the restoration of Abbey Dore is a statement by a man who
was affirming that the young Church of England was not a break with
what had gone before but a continuation of it. We know that he was
haunted with guilt about the lands he held and which, until the Dissolution,
had belonged to God; he was horrified by the spectacle of Dore Abbey
'altogether prophaned and applied to secular and base uses'. In the second
half of the sixteenth century, the relict of the parish church had been
used as a mere meeting house, and it comes as a shock to find it reclaimed
as sacred space and hence worthy of enrichment and adornment. Dore
Abbey illustrates that in the new century serious lines of division began
to open up around the Elizabethan Settlement of 1559. As a result what
congregations experienced by 1640 differed hugely from what had been
the norm at the end of the previous century.

By 1600, the Puritans, who aspired to further reform and more formal
links with their continental brethren, were still very much in evidence.

But their hopes that the new king James I, who had arrived from Calvinist Scotland, would move the Church of England in that direction had been dashed early in his reign at the Hampton Court Conference of 1604. The outcome was a firm rejection of the Puritan aspirations and the king's famous dictum: 'No bishop, no king.'

The Puritan faith was household-based: it saw the home as the seat of devotion, prayer and fasting. The Puritans had no time for the parish church other than as a place in which to gather to hear the Word of God. In church hats would be kept on; any convention of standing or bowing to say the Creed or in reverence to the Holy Name or Sacrament was ignored. The Puritans viewed many of the conventions that the Church of England retained as the dregs of popery, such as the sign of the cross at baptism, the wearing of a surplice or the churching of women. Along with that went a rejection of the structure of the Christian year: the Puritans acknowledged only Sunday, which was transformed into the Sabbath of the Old Testament, the day when everyone must rest and pass the time in prayer and listening to the Word. That equation had first been made by Nicholas Bound in *The Doctrine of the Sabbath* (1595) and was rapidly adopted. All sports were to be suppressed along with church ales, the ringing of bells and the whole cycle of rural festivities. Where a patron was powerful enough he could appoint a minister who would run the parish and its services in accord with Puritan principles. Where that didn't occur the godly increasingly took things into their own hands and went to a church outside their parish where their demands would be met.

The vast majority of parishes, however, can be described as run-of-the-mill conformist. Of course, Puritanism had had an enormous impact, and many Puritan views and beliefs had by 1600 become part of the mainstream, in particular their spiritual focus on hearing the Word from the pulpit, together with an increasing adoption of the Sabbatarian Sunday. But most believers also abided by – and loved – the Book of Common Prayer, which provided the framework for corporate worship in the parish church. They retained the cycle of the church year, and had no objection to the rites, ceremonies and attire laid down in the Prayer Book, nor to communal festivities like the Rogationtide beating of the parish boundaries, May Day or church ales. And they could react on occasion quite sharply to clerics who tried to take them in the Puritan direction. One such was Thomas Daynes, vicar of Flixton in Suffolk. Literate members of his congregation took their Prayer Books to church and started to list all the things he omitted: Daynes refused to use the sign of the cross in baptism or allow any godparents; he wouldn't wear a surplice, allow the churching of women or even pray for Queen Elizabeth as Supreme Governor. His congregation took action and had him ejected from his living; he, in turn, denounced them as 'papists and atheists'. What such stories tell us is that by 1600 there were parishes comfortable with a faith based on corporate worship as expressed in the Prayer Book services, and which had little time for predestination and the exclusivity of the godly. Yet their spiritual life too was based on the Word not the Sacrament.

For the man in the pew much that was to happen later in the century was foreshadowed in the 141 Canons passed under the influence of Archbishop Richard Bancroft (1544–1610) by the Convocations of Canterbury in 1604 and of York in 1606. Designed to spike the Puritans, these further defined the position of the young Church of England. The Canons decreed that no minister should depart from what was laid down in the Book of Common Prayer. Churchgoers should receive communion kneeling; they should also kneel for prayers and the litany and stand for the Creed. Men should doff their hats on entering church and everyone make 'lowly reverence' at the name of Jesus. Communion was obligatory for everyone over the age of sixteen at Easter. And, what was more, 'Every minister shall wear a decent and comely surplice with sleeves, to be provided at the charge of the parish.'

The Canons were never sanctioned by Parliament, nor do they seem to have been enforced. Even Archbishop Bancroft took a soft line and sought to implement them by debate and persuasion. On the whole, everything went on as it always had done except, that is, for one significant change: the publication of the Authorised Version of the Bible in 1611, commissioned by James I in the aftermath of the Hampton Court Conference. It was a revision of the earlier Bishops' Bible, and took into account both Protestant and Roman Catholic translations, but steered a path between the two. The result was a text of such powerful felicity that, along with the Book of Common Prayer, it has remained the bedrock of the Anglican tradition. Within a generation it was to become the most familiar, and often the only known, text of the Bible.

The Authorised Version of the Bible, 1611.

This seemingly tranquil scene would be disturbed when the young Church of England began to develop its own theological foundations. What set it apart was that it was not a branch of the reformed churches that had sprung up across Europe. It was, as its first archbishop, Matthew Parker (1504–75), had written, a continuum: not a break with the past but a return to the purity and traditions of the Early Church, before the arrival of the popish St Augustine. When the monarchy embarked on the Reformation, its priority was to return the nation to the pure faith of the Early Church.

As a result, Anglican theologians developed an intense interest in the works of the Greek and Latin Church Fathers. What they learned there about the Early Church was very different from what prevailed in the average post-Reformation parish with its increasingly Puritan ethos. They discovered a Christianity that stressed the importance of the sacramental life and venerated tradition. Moreover, patristic sources emphasised the inherent sanctity of both the consecrated place, the church, and the objects within it, like the altar.

The greatest patristic scholar, Lancelot Andrewes (1555–1626), bishop of Winchester, saw the Book of Common Prayer as a continuation of the teachings of the Greek and Latin Fathers. Through his studies he rediscovered the centrality of the sacraments, above all the Eucharist, which he didn't view as a merely commemorative act like the Puritans but one in which Christ was really present. From the Church Fathers too came a belief in the importance of ordered ceremonial in worship. All of this was to have a dramatic effect on the country church when, with the accession of Charles I in 1625, those who shared Bishop Andrewes's concept of the Church gained the ear of the king. During the preceding twenty-five years two increasingly antipathetic views, those of the Puritans and the new ceremonialists, had uneasily co-existed. Now the latter gradually gained episcopal dominance, culminating in the appointment of William Laud (1573–1645) as archbishop of Canterbury in 1633. All

Holy Communion, 1624.

that was incipient in the work of Andrewes and others, and which had begun to find legislative expression in the Canons of 1604, was now enforced under the aegis of government. The result was yet another transformation of the church building, almost as radical as that which had happened in the 1550s.

By that time patristic studies had led to a revaluation of both bishops and clergy. There was renewed emphasis on their ability to be a vehicle of supernatural, God-ordained, powers, which in the Eucharist could consecrate the bread and wine so that Christ was really present. As one patristic scholar wrote, 'the sacrifice of the altar . . . is the particular function of the priest to perform'. The priest's ability to bestow blessings, to sign a child with the cross and to give absolution were all viewed in a new light as the Church of England began to see itself as belonging to an ancient apostolic tradition rediscovered. Such a position led naturally to a very different view of the church, as the place where the sacraments were central and in which spirituality was expressed through corporate worship rather than verbal instruction.

As we have seen, the Book of Common Prayer was ambiguous as to the exact nature of the Eucharist. To the Puritans communion was a memorial act, an ordinary meal for which they either stood or sat; to them the Holy Table was just a table. But to Andrewes and his followers the Holy Table became once more the altar upon which Christ was present in a very real way. Hence it had to be placed where it could be accorded due reverence and was secured by means of rails from profanation. Steps should mark the approach and the table should be covered with a rich cloth falling to the ground. Both priest and communicants should kneel to receive and the Holy Table should be accorded a bow. We have returned to a world where physical objects are sacred.

Many more of Bishop Andrewes's beliefs would now find their way into the parish church. By 1700 we find two lighted candlesticks on the altar, the practice of the 'mixed chalice' of wine and water in the celebration of the Eucharist, the use of incense and the display of both Bible and Prayer Book in richly embroidered bindings on the altar. Moreover, the liturgy was conducted with stately decorum. In that it could draw on the ceremonial tradition preserved in Elizabeth I's Chapel Royal, which was developed when Andrewes was dean there from 1618 to 1626; here he brought its liturgical arrangements in line with his own ideals.

The reaching back to the past led to a very different way of looking at the church building. As the parish church had not been abandoned at the Reformation, it was now capable of embodying, in a physical sense, the continuity of the Church of England with the medieval church. Already in the 1590s, Richard Hooker, whose *Of the Laws of Ecclesiastical Polity* (1594–7) provided the Anglican Church with its theological foundations, saw the building in a new light. To him, the parish church was 'the house of prayer ... a court beautified, with the presence of the celestial powers ... here we stand, we pray, we send forth hymns to God, having his Angels intermixed as our associates'. For John Prideaux (1578–1650), Regius Professor of Divinity at Oxford, it was a holy space through 'Christ's promises, sacred meetings, united devotion [and] participation [in] ... the Word and Sacraments'. For William Laud it was 'the greatest residence of God on earth'.

Thus the building should be treated with reverence. It was to be restored and maintained in good order and, most of all, it should be made beautiful for we 'behold His glory and majesty in the stateliness and beauty of the building, in the richness of the sacred vessels and ornaments ... [and] the dignity, holiness and sacred pomp of His ministers'. Such a view is apparent in the various dedication services compiled by Andrewes for new churches. As a consequence, church buildings, many of which had begun to crumble by 1600, were back on the parish agenda. In 1603, the church at Upton-by-Southwell in Nottinghamshire, for example, was in an appalling state of dilapidation: the porch decayed, the floor still bare earth, the walls wringing wet and the windows broken. The following year saw the first of a long series of payments 'for the beautifyeing of the church'; in 1613 the floor was paved and a new pulpit arrived replete with a silk-fringed pulpit cloth; and by the 1630s the church conformed to every one of William Laud's liturgical demands.

After his appointment as archbishop of Canterbury in 1633, Laud became the driving force behind 'the general mending, beautifying and adorning of all English churches'. Already in October 1629 diocesan commissions had been set up to survey churches and order their repair. Church commissioners and impropriators were taken to court for the neglect of any building. The diocesan commissions were to see that both church and chancel were in good structural repair, that any pews which impinged on aisles or cross aisles should be demolished, and that any pews which impeded a view of the east end be reduced in height. All of this was done with a clear idea of how the interior should be arranged, moving in sequence from the font, sited near the west door, the scene of baptism and the reception of new members of the Church; along the centre aisle, with its focus on the pulpit from which the Word was expounded; and, finally, up through the screen into the chancel with the Holy Table, the setting for the celebration of the Eucharist.

Interior with pew rooms and a musician's gallery obscuring the chancel, St Michael, Rycote, Oxfordshire.

The desire to demonstrate the Church of England's continuity with the pre-Reformation Catholic Church, yet purged and reformed, was often emphasised by the deliberate use of the Gothic style, a conscious medievalism not only in architecture but in the design of any newly made altar vessels. Bishops strove to put an end to the use of any old jugs, bottles and plates in favour of proper plate. In the diocese of Peterborough, for example, every parish was ordered to buy a silver plate for the Eucharistic bread and a silver chalice for the wine. These were engraved with scenes and motifs reflecting the search for a recognisable Anglican design, with which to adorn and beautify both the interior and the artefacts used in worship. This quest too began in Andrewes's private chapel and found expression in his choice of New Testament scenes, such as the image of Christ as the Good Shepherd, the Star of Bethlehem or the proliferation of angels, from which sprang the winged cherubs' heads and celestial rays that would become the norm in churches built later in the century. This return to imagery and decoration began in the chapels of great houses, like Hatfield House, and the cathedrals, like Durham, but as time went on, it also spread into ordinary parish churches. At Burton Latimer, in the diocese of Peterborough, the altar rails were adorned with golden stars, and at Passenham, in the same diocese, the walls were painted with figures of the prophets and evangelists.

This revival of the visual was founded on a belief in what Laud called 'the beauty of holiness', a piety that contained a strong aesthetic element, casting the Church of England, in the words of George Herbert (1593–1633), as:

> A fine aspect in fit array,
> Neither too mean nor yet too gay,
> Shews who is best ...

It is an atmosphere Herbert caught in poems like 'The Church Floor':

> Mark you the floor? That square and speckled stone
> Which looks so firm and strong,
> Is Patience;
> And the other black and grave, wherewith each one
> Is checkered all along,
> Humility.
>
> The gentle rising, which on either hand
> Leads to quire above,
> Is Confidence;
>
> But the sweet cement, which in one sure band
> Ties the whole frame, is Love
> And Charity.

It is difficult for us to comprehend the electric effect that these developments had at the time. Historians remain divided as to how to interpret what happened during the first half of the seventeenth century; what they agree on is that the imposition of the ceremonialism that had its roots in Bishop Andrewes's chapel brought the Church of England into severe crisis. Some argue that the polarisation that occurred in the 1630s disturbed the previous 'Jacobean consensus'; others deny that such a consensus ever existed. As we have seen, the norms of behaviour in the parish church as laid down in the Canons of 1604 could easily be ignored – with or without the connivance of those meant to impose them. It was only after 1630, when the physical reordering of churches became mandatory, that trouble erupted and the Puritans were faced with what they regarded as the reintroduction of popery.

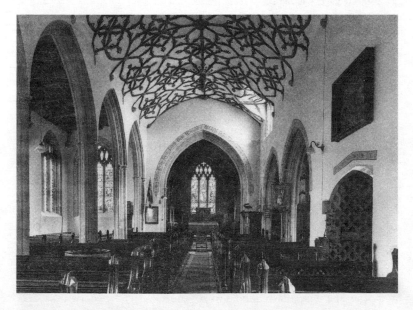

Anglican Gothic ceiling, St Mary, East Brent, Somerset, 1637.

The polarisation in the Church of England had already begun over the parishes' acceptance or rejection of the Church year. The Elizabethan settlement of 1559 had left the Catholic framework virtually intact except for the expurgation of certain holy and saints days, like Corpus Christi. To this was added a new regal cycle of festivals of state, such as Accession Day and 5 November, marking the failure of the Gunpowder Plot of 1605. The ecclesiastical year as a cyclical remembrance of the birth, life, passion and resurrection of Christ together with the coming of the Holy Spirit was rejected by the Puritans; to them only the Sabbath had to be observed.

The spread of Sabbatarianism resulted in the suppression of the sports and pastimes that had from time immemorial taken place on the village green after church. This led James I in 1618 to issue his *Book of Sports*, which ministers were instructed to read out to their congregations at Evening Prayer. It enjoined that

> . . . our good people be not disturbed, letted or discouraged from any lawful recreation, such as dancing, either men or women, archery for men, leaping, vaulting or any such harmless recreation, nor from having May games, Whitsun ales and Morris dances, and the setting up of Maypoles and other sports therewith used, without impediment or neglect of Divine Service: and that women shall have leave to carry rushes to the church for decoration of it according to the old tradition.

Most of this had already been spelled out in the Canons of 1604, but Puritans continued to close down local sports and revelry, and even when the *Book of Sports* was reissued in 1633, little headway was made in areas where Puritans had the ascendancy. Yet royal policy saw such activities as the secular equivalent of church attendance, twin aspects holding the parish community together in social harmony.

The jaws of Hell, St Peter, Wenhaston, Suffolk, fifteenth century.

St Michael, St Helen, Ranworth, Norfolk, fifteenth century.

Baptism, from the Seven Sacraments window at St Michael, Doddiscombesleigh, Devon, fifteenth century.

A funeral sermon being delivered in the church of All Saints, Faringdon, Berkshire, on the death of Sir Henry Unton in 1596. A unique record of a funeral procession making its way to a church decked in black, and in which the men sit on one side and the women on the other. In front is the magnificent tomb erected by Unton's widow.

Coming from Evening Church, 1830: Samuel Palmer's mystical vision
anticipates the renaissance of the country church.

The parson as gentleman: Wright of Derby's portrait of the
Reverend and Mrs Thomas Gisborne, 1786.

Slumbering in the pew, by Thomas Rowlandson, *c.* 1800.

YORKSHIRE DALES

A NATIONAL PARK AREA

'Across the glittering pastures
And empty uplands still
And solitude of shepherds
High on the folded hill'
  A. E. *Housman*

TRAVEL BY
TRAIN

Services and fares from Stations and Agencies

Icon of England: the village and its church. British Railways Poster, 1961.

Parish harmony and hierarchy was also reflected in church seating. As in previous periods, there could be ferocious disputes as to who sat where, which could escalate into exchanges of verbal abuse, blows and legal proceedings. In 1635 Richard Neile, archbishop of York, advised to steer clear of it all, to avoid the segregation of the sexes and regulated seating, as it 'will beget more brabbles, suits in law, & prohibitions, than either you or I would be contented to be troubled with'. But troubled with it he must have been, for the new directives from Canterbury ordered the clearing of naves, cross aisles and chancels of pews or encroachments; moreover, every pew was to be reduced to a height of three feet. Those who suddenly found their pew vanish or cut down would have been alienated by those new directives that advocated 'the beauty of holiness'.

These changes reflected a shifting emphasis on the church interior. Up until the 1620s, during a period that witnessed an evangelical drive based on sermons, the focus had been the pulpit. Huge numbers of country churches have Jacobean pulpits, handsome objects replete with a sounding board or tester to maximise audibility in a pre-microphone age. Numbers of licensed preachers rose during the first decades of the seventeenth century. In 1603 there were 920 preachers for 1,255 parishes, and regardless of what form of Protestantism a parish supported, lay activism and zeal centred on remembering the main structure and argument of the sermon. Those who were literate would make notes of what was said and discuss the content later in the day. But as we move into the late 1620s and early 1630s the emerging High Church party, made up of the followers of Bishop Andrewes committed to an elevated view of the sacraments and a belief in ordered ceremonial in worship, argued that 'the beauty of preaching had preached away the beauty of holiness'. Thus far tighter controls were introduced, controversial topics were forbidden and sermon length was curtailed to an hour's duration. There was to be no second sermon at evensong; instead, the young were to be catechised. Those licensed to preach at Divine Service could no longer do so without first taking matins and ante-communion wearing a surplice. Inevitably this flowering of the Church's latent Catholic traditions signalled a new divide between the wholly Scripture-based faith of the godly and that stemming from Cranmer, Jewel and Hooker, who drew on the teachings of the Early Church Fathers.

The greatest change, however, was to be the reordering of the chancel and the east end. Charles I saw himself as restoring the 'true former splendour of uniformity, devotion and holy order'. Alas, that was not how it was to be viewed in many churches when, in 1633, the king gave the ordinary, an ecclesiastic with power of jurisdiction, the ability to alter any internal arrangement contrary to the prescriptive rights of the congregation. This caused turbulence in some dioceses, but in others, such as Norwich, Ely and Peterborough, the king's instructions were strictly enforced. The Holy Table had to be placed permanently against the east wall in a north–south position; over it a carpet should fall to the ground and the area was to be railed in; and communicants henceforth should receive kneeling at it. This was a huge change. Many churches previously had the table in the chancel placed lengthwise with seating around it on three sides; in others, such as East Retford in Nottinghamshire, the table was too long and had to be shortened.

Nothing so systematic had been imposed since the middle of the previous century. All over the country there was a frenzy of activity as communion tables were adapted and moved; rails erected; surplices purchased along with pulpit cloths, covers for the altar, service books, pewter flagons for the communion wine, chests for books, alms boxes and cushions. To that we can add structural repairs to walls, roofs and porches, not to mention glazing broken windows, paving earthen floors and putting the bells in order.

Where such work was carried out, the result was a church interior that looked very different from the previous eighty years; in fact, it was more reminiscent of how churches had looked before the Reformation. This transformation was reinforced by the shift of attention from the pulpit to the altar and the imposition of a whole repertory of reverent and humble behaviour. By 1638 a zealous ceremonialist bishop like Richard Montagu made sure that visitations checked on a congregation's deportment: 'Doe your parishioners at their entrance within the Church doores use that comely and decent deportment which is fitting for God's house . . . do they uncover their heads, sit bare all service time, kneele downe in their seates, bowing towards the Chancell and Communion Table?' Did they 'bend or bow at the glorious sacred and sweet name of Jesus'?

Those committed to this transformation saw a Church reinvigorated, one in which preaching was no longer an end in itself but a means of guiding people to corporate prayer. Their vision was of a new public piety led by a clergy praying both with and for the congregation and dispensing to them sacramental grace. And to them it was through the timeless observation of the Christological cycle of the Church year that the members of the visible Church on Earth came closest to the Church triumphant in Heaven.

Alas, that vision was never widely shared. We know that the enforcement of 'the beauty of holiness' across the country was variable. As had happened so often previously, it could be got around or ignored in parts. But in many places it produced an uproar and in others a deep unease as to where all this was leading. What is so striking about the 1630s and 1640s is that for the first time – and unlike the 1540s and 1550s – we learn about the reaction from below, how the man in the pew felt about the changes thrust upon him. By 1635 in the parish of Beckington in Somerset, for example, the Holy Table had stood for seventy years 'in the midst of the chancel, enclosed with a very decent wainscot border and a door, with seats for the communicants to receive around it'. When the churchwardens refused to demolish it, they were excommunicated by the bishop; when they

Baptism, 1624.

appealed against him, they were thrown into prison. In the end they submitted, had to perform public penance and carry out the alterations.

Confrontations of this kind began to take place wherever the new ceremonialism came up against fierce resistance. In Northamptonshire Sir Nathaniel Brent demonstrated to his parishioners how to bow at the name of Jesus, 'the greatest matter they stick on'. In the diocese of Hereford the bishop insisted on the use of the sign of the cross at baptism and the wearing of a surplice but did not enforce bowing at the Holy Name. In April 1642 at a christening at Radwinter in Essex, someone confronted the minister 'by coming up close and standing in a manner by him, told him he should not have her [i.e. the child] out of her the godmother's arms, nor sign her with the sign of the cross; and to that end flung the cloth over the face of the child, keeping his hand vpon it, and saying, "It is the mark of the Beast."'

These lines of division foreshadowed the demise of the parish as a community that worked and worshipped together, united in a shared form of Christian faith. For centuries the parish congregation had been held together by the sense of the sacred and by rituals performed in church, which even the Reformation did not wholly shatter but reconstituted through the services of the Book of Common Prayer. Now the words of the Prayer Book guided that community through birth and death, procreation and salvation. The texts set out a shared moral code with formal rules of conduct which governed community relationships. Within these overall boundaries there was still a large degree of diversity; there was disagreement from time to time but as long as no firm line of conformity was drawn the fragile edifice was able to survive. However, when a specific interpretation of the Anglican tradition, regarded by many as nascent popery, sought to impose its will on every parish church in the country, the result was disaster.

When civil war came in 1642 the forces of destruction were to exceed any of the devastation to parish churches in the previous century. The survival of 'the beauty of holiness' created by Lord Scudamore at Abbey Dore is almost unique.

Chapter 6

Collapse and Fragmentation

THE CHURCH AT BRAMPTON BRYAN is sited at the northernmost tip of Herefordshire, close to that ancient seat of the government of the Marches, Ludlow. Although not particularly interesting in itself, what sets it apart is that it was rebuilt on the ruins of a medieval church by a Parliamentarian, Sir Robert Harley, in 1656, three years after Oliver Cromwell's assumption of the office of Lord Protector. Harley, together with his third wife, Brilliana, was a leading Puritan in a county that was the exact opposite: Herefordshire was conservative and Catholic in sympathy. In 1643, shortly after the outbreak of the Civil War, Harley committed himself to the Solemn League and Covenant, an alliance with the Scots designed to force Presbyterianism on to England. He also chaired the committee for the destruction of superstitious and idolatrous monuments in churches. It comes as no surprise that the church he began to build in the year he died was a meeting house for hearing the Word of God and, therefore, devoid of a chancel.

It was erected at a time when the Church of England had in effect been abolished, episcopacy banned and the Prayer Book forbidden. And yet the Gothic style of the church clearly echoes that of its hated Laudian predecessors. In the 1630s Sir Robert's mother, Lady Harley, had written to her son at Oxford bitterly criticising the Laudian innovations in ceremonial and church decoration. The interior of Brampton Bryan must have resembled a gloomy baronial hall with a pulpit and communion table; Harley would be horrified if he saw the interior as it is today, for in the 1880s arrived all the Laudian features he viewed as popery – steps up to an altar placed beneath the east window, communion rails and a font.

There is a counterpoint to Harley's church. In 1653, three years prior to the building of Brampton Bryan, the staunch royalist Sir

St Barnabas, Brampton Bryan, Herefordshire.

Robert Shirley, in direct defiance of the Parliamentarian regime, erected in his parkland a monument to seemingly vanquished Laudian ideals. The church at Staunton Harold in Leicestershire is also built in the Gothic style but it has the communion table – richly dressed, approached by steps and set within rails. It is sited in an empty chancel, the arrangement fully in accord with that we encountered at Lord Scudamore's Abbey Dore. Over the west door Shirley placed an inscription stating that he had erected the church during a time 'when all thinges Sacred were throughout the nation Either demolisht or profaned'. For this affront he was imprisoned.

The divisions within the Church of England had steadily worsened through the 1630s, and during the turbulent decades from 1640 to 1660 the country

Holy Trinity, Staunton Harold, Leicestershire: a Laudian ideal erected during the Interregnum.

was dragged into a bloody civil war between king and Parliament before becoming first a republic and later a protectorate. These decades were to take their toll on every parish in the land. This was a conflict about many things but a central issue was what form worship should take in parishes. As we have seen, the Church of England had been ambiguous and divided from its inception, and these divisions hardened when Archbishop Laud and others were seen to impose their vision of uniformity. When Charles I was reduced to summoning what became known as the Long Parliament in 1640, the overwhelmingly Puritan majority of the House set about reversing everything that had happened during the previous decade. Their aim was to impose a different uniformity on the national Church, based on godly principles. Their quest, like Laud's, was to end in failure.

Even before the Long Parliament could implement its decisions, there were outbreaks of violence in Puritan parishes. Communion rails were removed, sold or hacked to pieces; surplices were dragged off the backs of clerics and the Prayer Book snatched from their hands and torn up. In 1641 Parliament appointed commissioners whose task it was 'to demolish and remove out of all churches and chapels all images, altars, or tables turned altar-wise, crucifixes, superstitious pictures, and other monuments and relics of idolatry'. This gave official sanction to what was already happening in many Puritan parishes. Not everyone, however, caved in. The vicar of Furneaux in Hertfordshire 'walked the churchyard at night sword in hand, and said he would rather lose his life than let the rails be pulled'. And enough Caroline rails survive to indicate that across the country the reaction to this new iconoclastic wave was uneven.

We now witness a complete reversal of everything that had occurred between 1600 and 1640. During that time there had been a sustained effort to suppress the Puritan influence; now the godly fought back. Having gained power in Parliament and with the backing of a Parliamentary Army, they aimed to smash any allegiance to the Book of Common Prayer, to wipe out any vestiges of Catholic ceremonial and to destroy any images that still lingered in the parish churches. The Christological calendar with its feast days was to be abolished; the rites of baptism, the churching of women, marriage and burial were all to be reformed or discarded altogether. Parliament, and later the successive experiments in alternative government, first the Commonwealth and then the Protectorate of Oliver Cromwell, were driven by a millenarian vision – a belief that people were living at the end of time when the Last Days so vividly described in the Book of Revelation would become a reality. Christ in glory would come to his people, with England cast as the new Israel. Those brought up reading such texts with its apocalyptic prophecies saw them fulfilled during those years, which saw the head of a divinely appointed monarch fall on the scaffold in 1649 and the hand of Providence guide a triumphant Parliamentary Army to victory over royalist forces.

Initially, Parliament wanted to abolish episcopacy and bring the Church of England in line with Presbyterian Scotland, which had aided Parliament in the war against the king. An Assembly of Divines at Westminster decreed that the old parish system was to remain in place but that parishes were to be grouped into *classes*, which were responsible for ecclesiastical government and discipline. The *classes*, in turn, were grouped into provincial assemblies, one for each county and one for London, in each of which there sat a minister and two lay elders from every parish. Representatives from these assemblies then came together to form a national synod at the top. But little of this ever got off the ground, except in certain areas like Wiltshire and southeast Lancashire, where *classes* were formed. Only eight out of some forty English counties organised themselves in line with Presbyterian principles; twenty-four did not even bother to reply to Parliament – an index both of opposition and of the powerlessness of Parliament to impose its will.

Those in the Puritan Parliament, who wanted ecclesiastical power to pass entirely to the parish and its laity and called themselves Independents, eventually gained the upper hand when in 1647 Cromwell saw a toleration bill passed giving 'such as profess faith in God by Jesus Christ the right to exercise their religion even if it differed from that publicly held forth'. Cromwell had little time for ecclesiastical niceties: he was determined to prepare the way for the Lord by creating a godly society worthy to receive him. This resulted in a raft of legislation aimed at controlling people's private lives in both behaviour and thought: laws were passed against the misuse of Sunday, against adultery, swearing and blasphemy. When, after the abolition of the bishops and the Church courts, the whole ecclesiastical structure collapsed by the middle of the 1640s, the task of policing fell to the civil magistracy. Inevitably they failed and in 1655 Cromwell appointed major generals whose task it was both to oversee local government and to further virtue and godliness. Ale houses were now shut by the hundreds

Mutilated relief sculpture, St Cuthbert, Wells, Somerset.

and time-honoured Sunday games suppressed together with any celebrations of old Christian festivals such as Christmas. It appears that
none of this was at all popular.

The Puritan takeover soon made itself felt in the average parish church. In
August 1643 Parliament passed an ordinance ordering the destruction of
all candles, tapers and plate on communion tables, along with any crucifixes, images and superstitious objects related to the Virgin, the persons of
the Trinity or the saints. Two years later Parliament ordered the destruction of all vestments and any other 'popish' ornaments, such as screens,
organs and fonts. All of this was to reduce the parish church to the status
of the Puritan 'public meeting house'. Medieval churches were condemned
by clerics such as John Wells, the vicar of Tewkesbury, who regarded them
as 'built in the reign of popery and for the honor and adoration of saints
[it] was not built for the honor and service of God'. As a result, during
the Civil War churches served as prisons, stables, hospitals and storehouses.
In addition, visitations of commissioners set out to smash anything that
would remotely remind the congregation of its Catholic past.

In East Anglia that task was assigned to William Dowsing. His
notes on his progress through Cambridgeshire and Suffolk make chilling
reading. The following are typical entries from 1643 on two Suffolk
parish churches:

> Beccles, April the 6th. Jehovah's between Church and Chancel;
> and the Sun over it; and by the Altar, *My Meat is Flesh indeed,*
> *and my Blood is Drink* indeed. And 2 Crosses we gave order
> to take down, one was on the porch; another on the steeple;
> and many superstitious Pictures, about 40. – Six several
> Crosses, Christ's, Virgin Mary's, St George's and 3 more;
> and 13 crosses in all; and Jesus and Mary, in Letters; and
> the 12 Apostles.

The Souldiers in their passage to York turn unto reformers pull down Popish pictures, break down rayles, turn altars into Tables

The destruction of the 'beauty of holiness': a rare depiction of the demolition of a Laudian church interior.

Cochie, April the 6th. We brake down 200 Pictures; one Pope, with divers Cardinals, Christ and the Virgin Mary; a Picture of God the Father, and many other, which I remember not. There was 4 steps, with a Vault underneath, but the first 2 might be levelled, which we gave order to the Churchwardens to [do] so. There was many Inscriptions of JESUS, in Capital Letter, on the Roof of the Church, and Cherubims with Crosses on their breasts; and a Cross in the Chancel, all which, with divers Pictures, in the Windows, which we could not reach, neither would they help us to raise the ladders, all which, we left a Warrant with the Constable to do, in 14 days.

Although Dowsing is probably giving a much inflated account of what he had destroyed, a great deal must have gone. But one senses that this time parishioners were reluctant to co-operate in the purge. Moreover,

Dowsing's accounts show just how much of the Catholic heritage was left in the 1640s in spite of the purges of the 1550s and 1560s. Today it is impossible to disentangle what was destroyed in the sixteenth century and what was removed in the 1640s. It is highly likely that the destruction this time centred on images that were integral to the architecture of the church, such as stained-glass windows and relief sculpture, which had survived the destruction of the previous century.

The physical assault on the parish church was accompanied by a spiritual attack designed to obliterate the services and rituals enshrined in the Book of Common Prayer. The Prayer Book itself was banned in January 1645 and Parliament ordered that all copies were to be confiscated and burnt; those who continued to use it were to be imprisoned. Then, three months later, a *Directory of Public Worship* was issued. Running to a mere forty pages it laid down no definite liturgy but acted as a guide to what in effect were a series of virtually improvised services devoid of formal structure. The *Directory* advised on appropriate topics for prayer but provided no wordings; even the basic formularies, such as the Nicene and Apostles' Creeds, were not included.

With this came the imposition of the Puritan Sabbath. Sunday was to be a day spent in self-examination, meditation and prayer: 'all worldly business or our ordinary callings laid aside, as they may be impediments to the due sanctifying of the day when it comes'. This was to be 'a holy cessation ... not only from all sports and pastimes, but also from all worldly words and thoughts'. By the end of 1645 the feast days of the old calendar had all been abolished.

Although the Puritans wanted each parish to opt for the form of worship that suited it, the *Directory* was far from popular. It was met with prevarication and resistance throughout the country and eventually failed. The proposed changes were doomed to failure because there was no administration in place to impose them, and even those charged with enforcing them were reluctant to do so. All this revealed a deep residual loyalty to the Church of England and the Prayer Book.

THE
LAMENTABLE
COMPLAINTS
OF
NICK FROTH the Tapſter, and RVLEROST the Cooke.

Concerning the reſtraint lately ſet forth, againſt drinking, potting, and piping on the Sabbath day, and againſt ſelling meate.

Printed in the yeare, 1 6 4 1.

A publican and a cook lament the puritan Sabbath, from an anti-Puritan tract, 1641.

In the early 1640s ceremonialist clerics had been ejected from their livings by congregations dominated by Puritans; after 1645 action against clerics deemed as Laudian, anti-Parliament or poor preachers came from on high. Many of these deprivations were extremely unpopular, and the new incumbent imposed on the parish would often find the tithe withheld from him. There is no evidence, however, that anyone was ejected for using the Book of Common Prayer, celebrating Christmas or welcoming all to Holy Communion. And it appears that amidst the chaos there was much continuity: between three-fifths and two-thirds of clergy in post in 1642 were still in their parishes in 1649, the year of Charles I's execution. Many must have taken the line of the legendary vicar of Bray standing by his flock and bowing to the wind.

These deprivations did nothing to accelerate the arrival of a godly ministry worthy of the Second Coming. In 1654 Cromwell set up a national committee of 'Triers', drawn from various religious bodies, whose task it was to examine those whom a patron wished to present to a particular living or lectureship. But suitable candidates were thin on the ground, and they could include separatists like Fifth Monarchists, who believed in the imminent return of Christ to establish his reign on Earth, and Baptists, who rejected the baptism of infants because they saw the rite as a personal expression of belief. Many came forward who had already been ordained: although the episcopacy had been abolished in 1646, the surviving bishops continued to ordain priests in secret. The problem of how to provide a godly ministry for the whole country was in fact never solved and many parishes found themselves devoid of a cleric. At Caldecote in Cambridgeshire, for example, there was no priest between 1644 and 1650.

The Book of Common Prayer continued to be used in spite of every government ordinance, and there could be scenes such as that which took place in the church at Boothby Pagnell in Lincolnshire, where the living was held by the ousted Regius Professor of Divinity at Oxford, Robert Sanderson. Here soldiers 'would appear and visibly oppose him in the church when he read the Prayers . . . they forced his Book from him, and tore it, expecting extemporary prayers'. But Sanderson was undeterred and must have continued to use the Prayer Book from memory, for he was given a warning in 1650 not to use it too literally, indicating that one way round the ban was 'to make some little variation, especially if the Soldiers came to watch him'. In fact, the Prayer Book continued to be widely used, and even in areas where the *Directory* prevailed, Prayer Book services would be conducted in secret behind closed doors. Feasts too continued to be celebrated, although by 1650 they were observed by only 40 per cent of the population. It was this period which witnessed an unparalleled flowering of Anglican devotional literature and poetry by John Donne, George Herbert and Henry Vaughan. Only in the twentieth century did the divine revelations of the Herefordshire mystic Thomas Traherne come to light. Herbert, in his *A Priest to the Temple* (1652), outlined the duties of a country parson to his flock, while his friend Nicholas Ferrar revived an Anglican form of the religious life at Little Gidding, which the Puritans were to break up in 1646. All of these would be bulwarks of Anglican piety in the centuries to come.

But despite widespread resistance, it is undeniable that a huge dislocation occurred at parish level during this time, far worse than what had happened previously. Those who had lived through the Reformation, traumatic though these events may have been, could still have experienced some kind of continuity with what had gone before. The young Church of England had purveyed a form of Christianity that centred on the parish church, retained much of the old Catholic calendar, was still sacrament-based and carried over some of the rituals of the pre-Reformation era. During the Civil War years all this was rejected and action taken to obliterate it from the minds of the ordinary parishioner.

Although they were ultimately to fail, the radical reforms of the 1640s and 1650s created a dramatic break with the past. Parishes that up until then had survived intact despite differing views within their congregations now fell apart. It is during this period that we witness the dissolution of the parish as the sole unit of Christian worship. Until the 1640s the only members of the community not embraced by the ministrations of the parish priest had been the recusant Catholics, but with the dissolution of the old ecclesiastical structure, numerous sectarian groups began to emerge. The so-called Separatists had no place for the parish church and moved away to form congregations with like-minded believers from other parishes. Here we witness a dramatic re-conception of Christian life: differing fellowships of the Gospel replace the parish community united in worship. This marked the end of a single Christian community congregating in a single corporate building; in a sense the great age of the country parish church ended here in the middle years of the seventeenth century.

The Separatists created their own services and rites in direct counterpoint to those that were performed in the parish church. The Baptists refused to utter a prayer in the company of any regarded as 'unregenerate'. The Quakers took things even further, rejecting a faith based wholly on the Word of God for a belief in the manifestation of the Holy Spirit within the individual. In their community there was no room for either Prayer Book or *Directory* – or, indeed, any clergy. Moreover, the Quakers were opposed to social hierarchy and the hat was to be doffed to no man. Other groups of Separatists thrown up in the maelstrom of the 1640s and 1650s included Fifth Monarchists; Ranters, who denied the authority of Scripture, Creed and ministry; and Muggletonians, who rejected the doctrine of the Trinity. Their emergence marked the end of a single Church embracing the whole nation.

During those turbulent years, the vast majority of the population that was still loyal to the parish church faced additional disruption in their everyday lives. Baptism, marriage, the churching of women and burial – all milestones in the life of any ordinary villager – were either banned or altered beyond recognition. Once again, we witness here a much more radical break with the medieval past than what had occurred at the Reformation.

Baptism was the ritual through which an original sinner, an infant parishioner, became the recipient of God's Grace and joined the Christian community. In the Catholic Church it had been regarded as so essential to salvation that, if a newborn baby was weak, even the women assisting with the birth could baptise the child. Baptism was one of the two sacraments to survive the purges of the Reformation. In the late sixteenth and early seventeenth centuries, it generally took place two or three days after birth, the Prayer Book stipulating the following Sunday or holy day. Although stripped of most of its Catholic ritual the ceremony still indicated a mystical transformation and thus gave a strong sense of continuity with the medieval past. The child was immersed three times in the font – the pouring of water was only permitted if the child was weak – and signed with the sign of the cross on the forehead. Although vestments had been discarded the minister still wore a surplice for the ceremony. The Anglican position on the rite was defined in the Canons of 1604, where a stone font was also stipulated.

As with so much else at the time, this ceremony too was divisive. To the Puritans the cross was 'the mark of the beast' and of 'a harlot which stirreth up to popish lust'. As we have seen in the previous chapter, this could lead to confrontation at the font when Puritan parents presented a child to be baptised by a traditionalist cleric. But then, again, a blind eye could be turned to Puritan-dominated parishes, where baptism was administered from a basin of water set on the communion table, the sign of the cross omitted and no surplice worn.

The attack on the Prayer Book ritual began in 1644 with a demand that fonts be demolished and reached its apogee in the *Directory* of 1645, where baptism was no longer given any set ceremony and the minister was advised to use 'his own liberty and godly wisdom'. It only stipulated that water should be sprinkled on the child's face from a basin. This radical departure led to a steady rise in private baptisms where the old forms could be used in secret.

In the case of marriage the break with the past was to be even more radical. Marriage was the most important rite of passage in any parishioner's life, whereby a man became a husband and householder, and a woman a wife and housekeeper. Marriage had been a Catholic sacrament and, although it ceased to be one after the Reformation, in many ways it gained rather than lost in status.

The medieval rite had been governed by a strong sense of hierarchy. The gentry were married below the chancel, while for the lower orders the ceremony was conducted at the church porch. The service took place amidst a gathering of family, friends and neighbours. After the banns had been read thrice, the bride was 'given' to the groom by her father or by an adult friend. The couple held each other by the hand, and each took a pledge with the priest acting as mediator. Then the groom laid a ring along with a monetary offering on a dish or the Bible. After the priest had sprinkled the ring with holy water and blessed it, the groom placed the ring on successive fingers of the bride's left hand: on the thumb in the name of the Father, on the first finger in the name of the Son, on the second in the name of the Holy Spirit and, finally on the third finger where it came to rest with the word 'Amen'. The couple then entered the church for the nuptial Mass and blessing.

The Reformation introduced some changes but the core of the ceremony was left untouched. In a sense the rite was enhanced, for it was now conducted for *everyone* inside the church in the presence of the congregation. Marriage was also strengthened in another sense: with the dissolution of convents and the advent of married clergy, chastity no longer occupied the exulted status it had enjoyed previously. The Church of England retained many elements of the Catholic rite, such as the prohibited seasons for marriage (principally Advent and Lent), the use of the ring and, in the early stages of the Reformation, the celebration of the nuptial Eucharist. The banns too continued to be read but were now spread over three consecutive Sundays prior to the ceremony.

The Puritans had always objected to the ring and here too they found ways of avoiding its use; in the *Directory* the ring was finally abolished. But a far more revolutionary change was brought in eight years later by the Marriage and Registration Act of 1653. On the basis that there was no scriptural authority for a minister to marry people, this statute denied the Church the right to celebrate marriages and substituted instead a civil ceremony. Although the equivalent of the banns continued to be read, most of the time this took place no longer in the parish church but in the local marketplace, and the ceremony itself was now conducted by a Justice of the Peace. The act also stipulated that clerics had no authority to keep parish registers or, indeed, to bury the dead – all this was cast as evidence of the 'dregs of popery'.

Marriage was usually followed by childbirth. The Prayer Book retained the rite of churching and authorised a ceremony in which the mother was invited to the communion table for a short service of thanksgiving centred on the recitation of Psalm 121. Here an offering was also made, usually in the form of money or the chrisom cloth. The *Directory* abolished churching altogether, thus eradicating one of the few rites that focused on the female parishioner.

The *Directory* also gave short shrift to funerals and burial. Now even praying beside the corpse or at the graveside was banned for lack of scriptural authority; only 'meditations and conferences suitable to the occasion' were to be permitted. Of all the new directives this must have been the hardest for any bereaved person to come to terms with: without any words of comfort the corpse was more or less tossed into the grave. The old Catholic rituals of death had been rich and meaningful, the body being censed and sprinkled with holy water and surrounded by burning tapers. There was the Requiem Mass and many more Masses followed over the years to pray for the soul of the deceased. As we have seen, prayers for the dead and indeed any belief that the living could do anything to aid the departed were wiped out at the Reformation. But evidence shows that this had been difficult to enforce. In counties like Lancashire they were still praying for the dead in the 1590s, revealing that in spite of almost half a century after the introduction of the Prayer Book belief in purgatory had not gone away.

Although the Prayer Book service was bleak, it did provide a structure for burial. The corpse in its winding sheet, often placed within a reusable parish coffin, was borne to the church in a cart or parish bier covered with a hearse cloth. It was met at the church stile by the incumbent and led to the graveside. The body was then lowered and the unforgettable words uttered: 'Earth to earth, ashes to ashes, dust to dust, in sure and certain hope of resurrection to eternal life.' Those present cast earth on the corpse which was placed with the head eastwards and the face upwards in order

A corpse in a reusable coffin captures the bleak nature of the Interregnum funeral.

to greet the angel at the day of resurrection. The churchyard too remained a sacred space in which resided the community of Christians departed. In the 1640s most of that reassuring ritual was abrogated and replaced by what amounted to a brutal burial.

But at parish level the administration of Holy Communion was to become the most divisive of all the changes introduced by the Puritans. Prayer Book traditionalists regarded communion, now increasingly an annual event celebrated at Easter, as an outward sign of neighbourly love and unity, with only the most scandalously unrepentant being refused the sacrament. From the outset, Puritans regarded such a generous bestowal of communion as 'promiscuous'. The *Directory* now turned the communion service into a commemorative event to which only the elect should be admitted. The Real Presence of Christ was firmly rejected and any form of sanctifying and blessing the elements of bread and wine banned. Those wanting to receive the sacrament were to be examined by the minister and two church elders, and only when they were thought fit were admitted to the Lord's Supper where they were to 'orderly sit about' or 'at' the communion table.

The new directives caused division in every church and it is hardly surprising that less than 20 per cent of parishes went in for what became known as 'closed communion', in which only the godly were seen as fit to receive. The new regime created an exclusive spiritual community where only the elect were destined for salvation. The parish church now became the domain of those deemed regenerate; the unregenerate had to look on as the chosen ones partook of the Lord's Supper. It is not surprising that the celebration of Holy Communion went into sharp decline during the 1650s; in some parishes it didn't happen at all. It appears that the reasons for this were complex: some parishes lacked the mechanism for detailed spiritual examination, but for most there was a real fear of the social division that such an exercise would perpetrate on a small rural community. And the ministers no doubt feared that those parishioners who were denied communion would refuse to pay their tithe.

Where 'closed communions' occurred it must have been devastating for those who were rejected. In the village of Marbury in Essex in 1654, the minister refused to celebrate the Lord's Supper at all because he deemed no one worthy enough to receive it.

In the long run it was inevitable that there would be a strong reaction against perpetually living in a world turned upside down where all systems of belief and structures of authority were challenged and demolished. After the death of Oliver Cromwell in 1658, this terrifying instability created a longing for the return of the old order and a casting of the pre-Civil War period as a lost golden age. The Civil War and the Interregnum had failed to obliterate the Book of Common Prayer; in fact, they sanctified it, so much so that it was to remain virtually unaltered until very recently. It had become part of popular culture, a new traditional religion replacing the Catholic faith. When the monarchy was restored in 1660, the Prayer Book, with its mid-sixteenth-century English, was already archaic but it had become untouchable.

The price paid for these decades of turmoil and bloodshed was a nation and a Church divided. In the parish church henceforth assembled only those who belonged to the Church of England and whose faith was expressed in the Book of Common Prayer. Many, however, went elsewhere.

Chapter 7

The Parting of the Ways

IT WAS A PAINTER FRIEND who introduced me to the church at Mildenhall, a village set in the leafy downlands east of the Wiltshire market town of Marlborough. Nothing about its exterior prepares you for what is to come on opening the door, for without this is like hundreds of other medieval village churches, a comforting patchwork of flint and stone with elements stretching from the thirteenth century to the time of the Reformation. It is the interior that comes as a shock, for we walk into a setting worthy of Jane Austen's Miss Bennet and Mr Darcy with Mr Collins presiding in the pulpit and the icy glare of Lady Catherine de Bourgh in a pew opposite.

Mildenhall is one of the few churches that escaped the hand of the Victorian improver. Inside it is all of a piece, exactly as it was in the year after the battle of Waterloo and the triumph of Britain as a world power. An inscription in the chancel records the renovation: '1816 This Church deeply in decay has been all but rebuilded generously and piously at their own expense' – 'their' being the churchwardens and other wealthy parishioners whose names follow.

The style is Gothic and everywhere one looks there are little pierced and embattled gables and ogees – Strawberry Hill come to Wiltshire. The decorations are either appliquéd or carried out in fretwork over the pews, pulpit and reading desk, and the musician's gallery at the west end. In the chancel the altar is backed by an elaborate reredos bearing the Decalogue flanked by the Creed and the Lord's Prayer. Here, a century and a half on from the depredations of the Interregnum, we see a church arranged in a manner Archbishop Laud would have applauded: rich in outward vesture and the chancel set apart as a sacred place, with the altar railed in. We seem to have gone into sharp reverse from where we left the average country church in

St John the Baptist, Mildenhall, Wiltshire.

the 1650s. And it is that reversal which makes the eighteenth century so fascinating.

In 1660 there was widespread weariness after two decades of political upheaval and social dislocation. The initial desire to accommodate both Presbyterians and Independents in a new settlement was strongly resisted by the returning Anglican clergy who were determined that the Puritans should never again exert power. The 1662 Act of Uniformity imposed on all parishes a slightly revised Book of Common Prayer, and every incumbent had to take an oath of loyalty both to the Prayer Book and to the monarchy. Two thousand ministers refused and were ejected from their livings. The Conventicle Act of 1664 banned meetings of more than four worshippers unless the Prayer Book was used, and in 1665 the Five Mile Act forbade ejected clergy to come within five miles of the place where they had held a living. It was a defining moment for the Anglican Church.

But the threat to the Church now seemed to come from a different direction. Both Charles II (reigned 1660–85) and his successor James II (1685–8) were known for their Catholic sympathies, the latter converting to Rome. We must remember that all through this period and well into the early eighteenth century ran a rabid and often totally irrational fear of Catholicism – a spectre that had its roots in the reign of Elizabeth and in such legendary events as the defeat of the Spanish Armada and the Gunpowder Plot, which became part of a Protestant national mythology. It would be fuelled in the eighteenth and early nineteenth centuries by almost continuous war against the Catholic superpower of France, first under Louis XIV and later under Napoleon.

The early years of the Restoration were a time of persecution for Nonconformists and Dissenters – the blanket terms now applied to Protestant groups who remained outside the national church – and both Charles and James realised that the only way to achieve toleration for Catholics was to guarantee toleration for Dissenters. Thus in 1672 Charles issued a Declaration of Indulgence by which Presbyterians, Congregationalists and Baptists could apply for licences to practise their faiths publicly at specified locations, and Catholics were allowed to worship in private. But Parliament was outraged and forced the king to cancel the Declaration the following year. James II took things much further in April 1687 when he too issued a Declaration of Indulgence for England and Wales, suspending all penal laws against Nonconformists. He then set out to repeal the Test Act of 1673, which required all officers to receive communion according to the usage of the Church of England, and much to the dismay of the Anglican establishment Catholics and Dissenters now began to be appointed to official positions. These developments precipitated the revolution of 1688, which brought in William

III – husband of James's daughter, Mary – and Mary herself as king and queen, and forced the Stuarts into exile. In terms of religion, this complex political story came to an end with the Toleration Act of 1689, which officially recognised Dissenters – except those who did not believe in the Trinity – who were allowed their own meeting houses. But the discriminatory conditions of the Test Act returned and Catholics continued to be excluded from a toleration that only embraced Protestants.

This brief summary must suffice to describe what happened at the top. But what took place in the thousands of country churches scattered the length and breadth of England? Recent historical studies have cast the whole period of the Reformation, which lasted from the 1530s until the middle of the seventeenth century, as a clash of cultures in which an educated Protestant élite, made up of the gentry and the new professional classes, took over the parish churches. They suppressed the folkloristic Catholic religion of the congregations inside, and, at the peak of their power during the Interregnum, they moved on to abolish its secular manifestations outside, such as church ales, May Day celebrations and games on Sunday. But when they lost their position at the Restoration, the use of the Prayer Book was rapidly re-established without any resistance, and the old folk festivals were immediately revived.

Yet after 1660 clerics were faced with congregations consisting not only of those who had remained loyal to the Book of Common Prayer but also including Quakers, Baptists, Congregationalists and members of numerous other sects that had emerged during the turbulent 1640s and 1650s, all objecting to episcopacy and the Prayer Book. How this difficult situation was handled depended on the incumbent. Some were the willow, allowing the Puritans in their flock to receive communion standing; others the oak, refusing to permit any variation from the the Prayer Book. In the early years of the Restoration some parishioners would worship both in their parish church and in a conventicle, and although there was an official drive to prosecute Dissenters, this rarely happened as people tended to protect their neighbours and fellow villagers.

Thus, during the early years of the Restoration, we witness power struggles within every parish church. The Act of Uniformity of 1662 ended that period of flux by defining Anglicanism as adherence to the letter of the Book of Common Prayer. With the enforcement of the act began the great parting of the ways which would affect every parish church: for the first time it was officially recognised that religious congregation and local community were no longer synonymous. God could no longer be found only in the parish church but wherever a fellowship of like-minded believers would assemble.

The existence of a group of people who worshipped outside the local church inevitably produced a sense of unease among those who looked to the parish church for spiritual and ethical guidance. As a result, the Church of England would turn in on itself, permitting not the slightest deviation from the Book of Common Prayer. More than ever before the Church became the arm of government, for religious dissent would now be associated with the turmoil of the Commonwealth and Protectorate. The display of the royal arms over the chancel arch became ever more meaningful, and great stress was laid on the celebration of royalist feast days, such as those marking Charles I's martyrdom or Charles II's escape after the battle of Worcester. The ghost of the Civil War was to haunt England throughout the eighteenth century.

After the Toleration Act of 1689, however, people could no longer be forced to attend the parish church: the Church of England had lost its mandatory hold on the nation. With worshippers free to choose between parish church and meeting house, to a large degree the Church's future now depended on the quality of its clergy. Anglican ministers were faced not only with holding on to their existing flock but persuading those who had left and joined other denominations to return to the fold. According to recent research, they seem to have been remarkably successful, for there were far fewer Dissenters at the close of the eighteenth century than at the beginning.

The Church realised that its future depended on educating both clergy and laity. This was the time of the religious societies and those dedicated to the reform of manners and morals, which were universally seen as being in a dire state. The most important of these was the Society for Promoting Christian Knowledge (SPCK), founded in 1698 'to promote and encourage the erection of charity schools in all parts of England and Wales; to disperse, both at home and abroad, Bibles and tracts of religion; and in general to advance the honour of God and the good of mankind ...' By the close of the eighteenth

Receiving Holy Communion, 1693.

century half the parishes of England had a charity school, and, for the first time, a large percentage of the congregation could actually read the Bible and the Book of Common Prayer. Thanks to the SPCK religious literature for the laity arrived in the churches, as well as libraries aimed at improving the pastoral abilities of the clergy; poor incumbents were aided by the Parochial Libraries Act of 1709, encouraging the formation of parish libraries. Often these came about through bequest: the rector of Crundale in Kent, for example, left to his church in 1729 no less than 195 folios, 161 quartos and 464 octavos.

The climate of conflict typical of the seventeenth century gradually gave way to the Age of Reason. The average incumbent now began to recognise both Dissenters and Catholics as his fellow Christian brethren, and even the warring parties within the Church of England came together to promote Christian morality, a belief in kindness to neighbours, the importance of sexual continence and the necessity of respect for the social order.

In the country parishes we now enter a period, described as 'the long eighteenth century', that stretches well into the Victorian age, and which is marked by the manifest alliance between the returned royalist gentry classes and the Established Church. The gentry supported the parish church and, in return, the clergy helped maintain the existing social and political order. In literature this relationship is vividly caught in the figure of Sir Roger de Coverley, the prototype country gentleman created by Joseph Addison in the *Spectator* in the early eighteenth century, whose exit from the family pew on Sundays precipitated the entire congregation rising to form an avenue of bowing and curtsying villagers. But living as we do in a post-deferential age, it is important to grasp that this was not as subservient as it would seem. The village as a living community was an essay in reciprocity. At the top came the gentry, men like Sir Roger, substantial landowners who exercised authority within the locality, and who as JPs or MPs represented its interests at the centres of power. As impropriators and patrons of advowsons, the gentry 'owned' the parish church more than at any other period in its history. The officiating cleric would have owed his position to Sir Roger and those who made up the avenue would have been his tenant farmers and workers on his estate.

The gentry also dominated the space within the church, its walls increasingly adorned with plaques commemorating members of the leading families, and their family pews taking precedence over any other seating. The mass reordering of churches in the nineteenth century has largely obliterated this hierarchical orchestration of the church's internal space, ranging from box pews allocated to wealthy families – whose comforts could even include a fireplace – to the benches for labourers at the back. Richard Gough's *Observations concerning the Seates in Myddle and the families to which they belong* (1701) gives us a vivid portrait of those who made up the congregation of a late seventeenth-century country church. Gough provides us with the history of each of the families which occupied pews in the church at Myddle, a parish a few miles north of Shrewsbury. He describes how the entire body of the church was arranged in pews to reflect the hierarchy of local families. But he also records the other internal changes affecting this country church. His description opens with the arrival of the Laudian communion table and altar rails, the old table being given to the schoolhouse. Gough goes on to recount how by order of Parliament in 1643 the rails were demolished, the chancel levelled and the communion table placed in the middle of the floor. It was not long before that relic of the Laudian beauty of holiness was replaced by 'a long one and two joined formes for the communicants to sitt att the table'. It appears that the donor of these made off with the Laudian altar. At the Restoration the rails returned and there was a new communion table – in Gough's opinion 'the worst of the three'.

It was those who came immediately below the gentry in rank, the major tenant farmers, who held office as churchwardens: they saw that the church was kept in good repair, managed the finances and were responsible for making presentations at visitations. Office was generally held for a period of two or three years, so that in the long run most influential families in the local community took part in running the church. Form and frequency of episcopal or archidiaconal visitations, when the bishop or the local archdeacon scrutinised the church's services, the maintenance of the building and other relevant matters, varied from diocese to diocese. Before each visitation in Norfolk during the eighteenth century, for instance, the archdeacon would issue a book of articles to each parish listing what he needed to know – 'Concerning the Church, Churchyard, Houses, Glebes and Tithes belonging to the Church', 'Concerning Ministers', 'Concerning Parishioners', 'Concerning Incest, Adultery, Fornication, etc'. By 1800 this extensive list had dwindled to a simple questionnaire concentrating on items such as fabric and furnishings and the order of worship, which was just filled in by the churchwardens. This reflected a shift in the control of parish morality away from the church; it had now become the business of the civil courts. The Church courts, which had returned in 1660, went into sharp decline when their prime role of correcting religious – and thus political – dissent was eroded by the Toleration Act of 1689.

As we move through the eighteenth century, the clergy start to emerge as a distinct social and professional group. Their income varied across the country, the average in Norfolk being £70, and in Wiltshire, at the close of the seventeenth century, just over £80. Many, however, were extremely poor: over half the livings in England in 1736 were below the poverty line of £50 per annum. Consequently a fund known as Queen Anne's Bounty was created in 1704 with the sole purpose of augmenting the livings of the poorer Anglican clergy. Pluralism, the holding of several livings by one cleric, was another solution to the problem of poorly endowed parishes, resulting in incumbents riding to and fro between two neighbouring parishes. Sometimes, if a cleric

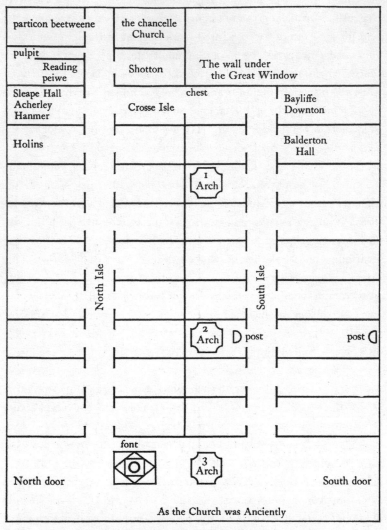

Seating in the church at Myddle, Shropshire, 'Anciently' and in 1701.

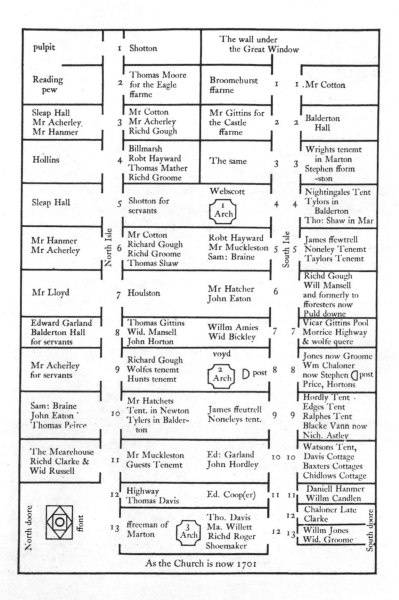

held several benefices, he would employ a curate in some of them, a custom that resulted in growing non-residence. In the diocese of Winchester this affected 26 per cent of parishes in 1725, 47 per cent in 1765 and 51 per cent in 1788. The demographic shift during the last quarter of the eighteenth century, through massive urbanisation in response to the industrial revolution, was never addressed by the Church, the distribution of both clergy and churches remaining hugely uneven and essentially medieval.

It is hardly surprising that the glebe and the tithe continued to form an important part of the clergy's income. In Norfolk the average glebe ran to thirty-nine acres, most of which was farmed and afforded much that made a parsonage self-supporting in terms of poultry, fruit and vegetables. The tithe was a permanent bone of contention as Dissenters had to pay it despite the fact that they lived without the cleric's minis-trations. This resulted in numerous court cases but the tithe was regarded as essential to supplement the clergy's income and the two Tithe Acts of 1696 enforced payment, giving the minister the right to recover up

Two villagers present their tithe, late eighteenth century.

to £10 of the tithe from Quakers by resorting to two JPs to enforce payment. By the end of the eighteenth century the tithe gradually ceased to be paid in kind and became a money transaction.

Most clergy lived on the level of a yeoman farmer but the more prosperous among them began to appear on local commissions for the land tax and of the peace, and from the last decades of the eighteenth century the number of clergy sitting on the bench or acting as JPs steadily rose. This would set them further apart from the congregation they served. The eighteenth century ushered in the era of the 'squarson', an incumbent who was less a cleric than a country gentleman, living a life of cultured leisure and country sports, whose flock were treated rather like dependants on a great estate. Although in theory a clerical career was open to all, increasingly the richer benefices became so desirable that the aristocracy and gentry, who held many of the rights of presentation to livings, began to colonise them for their younger sons. This is the world we catch in Jane Austen's novels.

Indeed, Jane Austen herself provides a perfect illustration of this world. Her family connections alone, excluding any ties of friendship, paint a vivid picture of the clerical dynasties whose interrelationship through common ancestry and cousinage guaranteed entry to the old universities as well as access to other influential families. Her father, the Reverend George Austen, was rector of Steventon on the north border of Hampshire. George himself owed his position to the patronage of a wealthy second cousin, Thomas Knight, who held extensive lands in Hampshire. George's wife, Cassandra, was the daughter of the Reverend Thomas Leigh, fellow of All Souls and rector of Harpsden in Oxfordshire. Cassandra's sister, Jane, married the Reverend Dr Edward Cooper, fellow of All Souls and rector of Whaddon and Sonning, and their son Edward later became rector of Hamstall Ridware. Cassandra's grandmother had been an aristocrat, a sister of the first duke of Chandos, and another one of her descendants was the Reverend Thomas Leigh, rector of Adlestrop, who was to inherit the huge family estate of Stoneleigh Abbey. George and Cassandra had eight children and, following a common practice in clerical families, sent two sons, James and Henry, into the ministry. Another son, Edward, was to marry the sister of three clergymen.

This tradition continued unquestioned for a long time and effectively eliminated any possibility of anyone from the lower classes joining the clergy. We seem to enter an age where the clergy became almost a caste consisting of clerical dynasties. The Wardes at Yalding in Kent held the parish from 1759 for a century, the Duncombes at Shere in Surrey from 1658 to 1843, and the Hanburys at Church Leighton in Leicestershire from 1753 to 1899. These may be unusual cases, but the Austen family provides abundant evidence that even if the same parish was not passed on from one generation to the next the profession most certainly was.

To be ordained clerics required a degree from one of the two universities, and scholarships were bestowed primarily on those who could claim kinship with a founder. (In the case of Jane Austen's family, her two brothers could claim descent, through their mother, from Sir Thomas White, founder of St John's College, Oxford.) The laity now expected their vicar to be a scholar who prepared his sermons in his study. George Herbert had written in the previous century that a parson should be well read in divinity, as well as in law and medicine, in order to help his parishioners. In practice, however, many clergy merely purchased a book of sermons by some well-known divine and read them out in the pulpit on Sunday. We must remember, however, that most degrees focused on the Greek and Latin classics and that few clerics specialised in divinity; in short, Georgian clerics were untrained in theology and in the elements of the spiritual life. The result was the virtual absence of what we know as pastoral ministry.

In his *Discourse of the Pastoral Care* (1692), Gilbert Burnet, bishop of Salisbury, had advised the cleric that 'His friends and his Garden ought to be his Chief Diversions, as his Study and his Parish, ought to

A JOURNEYMAN PARSON GOING ON DUTY.

A MASTER PARSON RETURNING FROM DUTY.

The poor curate and the prosperous parson, late eighteenth century.

be his chief Improvements.' The incumbent's task, Burnet wrote, was to administer the sacraments, deliver sermons, teach the catechism, visit the sick, and conduct burials and churchings. He was also to set an example to his flock in his own life, to show that godly attitudes had been subsumed into Anglicanism. The best way, he believed, to bring back Dissenters was through a clergy who 'were stricter in our lives, more serious and constant in our labours, and studied more effectually to reform those of our Communion, than to rail at theirs'. Even though his book remained popular, it appears that by the end of the eighteenth century Burnet's advice had been forgotten. Indeed, in the opening decades of the next century complacency was so commonplace that one historian has categorised the period as 'the age of negligence'.

The delightful diaries of the Norfolk cleric, Parson James Woodforde, paint a vivid picture of the comfortable life of a parson in the eighteenth century. This diary runs from 1758 to 1802 and, even in its contracted form, fills five published volumes. The parson also belonged to one of those clerical dynasties I have described above: his father was the rector of Ansford and vicar of Castle Cary in Somerset, his grand-father was rector of Epsom and his uncle, John, rector of North Cary, Somerset. Educated at Winchester and New College, Oxford, Woodforde was ordained in 1764, although it was not until 1776 that he came into the living of Weston Longueville in Norfolk, which he held until his death. Woodforde never married and a niece, Nancy, looked after his household. With an annual income of £400 Woodforde was able to keep two maidservants, two menservants, a boy and three horses. His two great passions were tending his garden and coursing fine, large hares with his greyhounds, named Duchess, Hector and Reach-em. This was a kindly man, generous to his parishioners, sending baskets of apples and veal broth to the poorest, alms to the old and bestowing a few pence on all the children in the village each St Valentine's day.

There is much delight to be found in his diary with its record of the minutiae of late Georgian rural life and its excessive preoccupation with every meal. Its very repetitiveness emphasises the tranquillity of such a rural existence, so far removed from clerical life in the twenty-first century. The entry for every Sunday is virtually always the same: 'Read Prayers and Preached this morning at Weston.' He usually notes which people from the great house were present, and occasionally whether the congregation was large or small. In accord with Georgian Anglicanism he marked both the Gunpowder Plot and the execution of Charles I with a service and also held one to celebrate the restoration to health of George III. It is difficult to work out the size of his congregation but on 27 February 1785, a day that saw hard frost and bitter wind, he noted that it was small – 'not 20 Persons there'. The service was conducted in the morning or in the afternoon, and as Woodforde got older he had to call on a curate to take it for him. On 12 June 1796 he noted that there was no service at Weston as the curate had to ride to three other churches to take theirs! Woodforde's diaries are wholly devoid of any mention of study, preparation of the sermon or pastoral care of a kind we would recognise today. What went on in the church every Sunday must have been a repetitious ritual to be endured. No wonder that the few images we have of actual services in action during that period depict most of the congregation slumped asleep with the boredom of it all.

As we have seen, the Church of England had always regarded itself as the old pre-Reformation Church restored to its pristine purity before the corruptions of Rome. Inevitably this perception led to intense study of the Early Church, and its buildings and liturgy were called upon to justify Anglican Church architecture and ritual, like the ceremony of the Eucharist. The definitive liturgical commentary of the eighteenth century, Charles Wheatly's *The Church of England's Man's Companion, or, A Rational Illustration of* . . . *the Book of Common Prayer* (1710), reveals how High Church clerics saw the communion service. Of the interior arrangement of the parish church in the eighteenth

Matth XVIII. 10. 20. 1.Cor. XI. 23. 24. 25. 26.

Holy Communion, from Charles Wheatly, *A Rational Illustration of the Book of Common Prayer*, 1714 edition.

century, Wheatly wrote: 'The nave was common to all people, and represented the visible world; the chancel was peculiar to priests and sacred persons, and typified heaven: for which reason they always stood at the east end of the church, towards which part of the world they paid a more than ordinary reverence in their worship . . .' He pointed out that in the Early Church Christians had turned eastwards in prayer, the direction of the coming of Christ, the true Sun of Righteousness; the Anglicans now followed their example. Wheatly argued that the positioning of the minister at the north end of the altar also echoed early Christian practice, although evidence suggests that in practice clerics in the eighteenth century faced both north and east when celebrating the Eucharist.

After the Restoration the arrangement of church interiors began to reflect the centrality of the Eucharist in Anglican worship. Alhough there were High and Low Church views as to what exactly happened at the moment of consecration, both sides essentially upheld the Real Presence of Christ. As we have heard from Wheatly, the division between the nave and the chancel represented a very real theological statement, which set the Church of England apart from both Roman Catholics and Dissenters. The altar rails, which had been such a bitter bone of contention in the 1630s, now became universal, and the altar within was often raised and always covered with a rich cloth; sometimes it was also adorned with candlesticks and a display of plate. The reredos framing the words of the Decalogue, Lord's Prayer and Creed became increasingly elaborate, with an abundance of celestial rays and triangles for the Trinity. Painted altarpieces also began to make their appearance.

Many features that the Victorian reformers were to cast aside as emblems of the ungodliness of the previous century were uncontroversial at the time. The royal arms sited over the chancel arch, for instance, caused no concern in an age that still regarded the monarch as a 'spiritual person', someone who had been anointed and clothed in a dalmatic at his coronation and, although not ordained, was capable of jurisdiction in spiritual matters. Another artefact which was anathema to the Victorian Tractarians, the three-decker pulpit, was also seen to continue the practice of the Early Church where its equivalent had been the ambo. 'The *Ambo* itself,' wrote Joseph Bingham, author of *Origines Ecclesiasticae: or, The Antiquities of the Christian Church* (1708–22), 'was what we now call the Reading-Desk, a Place made on Purpose for the Readers and Singers, and such of the Clergy as ministered in the first Service, called *Missa Catechumenorum.*'

Surprisingly, images also returned to church interiors in the eighteenth century. William Wake, archbishop of Canterbury, had written in his *Exposition of the Doctrine of the Church of England* (1686) that 'we will respect the Images of our SAVIOUR and the blessed VIRGIN. And as some of us now bow down before the Altar, and all of us are enjoined to do so at the Name of the LORD JESUS, so will we not fail to justify all due respect to his Representation.' In this way began the return of pictorial art to the parish church.

But despite the return of 'the beauty of holiness' to church interior and service, what the average parishioner experienced on Sunday seems hardly inspiring. Challenged first by Dissent and then by Methodism, the clergy became increasingly defensive, determined to maintain a hold over the liturgy and regarding the services of the Prayer Book as sacrosanct. After the turbulent years of Civil War and Interregnum they were deeply resistant to any kind of lay participation and suspicious of any spirituality expressing itself outside the walls of the parish church. All of this explains the appeal of John Wesley and the Methodist movement. From the 1730s Wesley offered a more personal faith, allowing emotions that were vividly expressed in the hymns sung at Methodist meetings held across the country. Today we sing them without thinking but they were beyond the pale to any eighteenth-century incumbent. They range from 'Hark the herald angels sing!' to

Rejoice the Lord is King,
Your Lord and King adore;
Mortals, give thanks and sing,
And triumph evermore:
Lift up your hearts, lift up your voice
Rejoice, again I say, rejoice.

Wesley remained an Anglican to the day he died, but when he began ordaining ministers himself in 1784, the spiritual renewal he had started within the Church of England became a separate denomination.

Not everyone attended church any more in Georgian England, but enough pressure was still in place to make it likely that almost all did, as attendance was both a spiritual and a social statement. Gathered into the building on Sunday was virtually the entire local community, seated in pews whose arrangement replicated the hierarchical structure of

Matins in a country church, 1790.

society. Not every church had box pews for families; in some churches the old medieval arrangement continued with men sitting in front and women behind, or men and women on either side of the central aisle, men to the south and women to the north. But the trend now was towards seating 'according to their qualities and due respects' or 'according to their degree, ability and calling', which took into account marital status, age, wealth and contributions to the parish rates. Some

The church divided into an area for the Word and one for the Sacrament, St John the Baptist, King's Norton, Leicestershire, 1757–75.

parishioners purchased a life-interest in a pew, others rented them on an annual or quarterly basis.

The two services on Sunday were Morning Prayer at 10 a.m., consisting of matins, litany, ante-communion and sermon, and Evening Prayer at 3 p.m., which was a shorter ceremony without sermon or litany. Morning Prayer was long and repetitive: it included four Bible readings and the Lord's Prayer was said as many as five times. Lay participation had been reduced to a minimum – during Morning Prayer 3,500 words were spoken by the minister and only 700 by the congregation – and that exclusion of the laity explains the enormous popularity of psalm singing, which was virtually the only opportunity of active participation open to parishioners.

The evidence we have on sermons is contradictory. The fact that the clergy were now more educated meant that their sermons – or the ones they read but were written by others – often went straight over the heads of their listeners, and visitation reports reveal the gulf between the cleric and his audience. Oliver Goldsmith, author of *The Vicar of Wakefield* (1766), not himself a cleric, described the average eighteenth-century sermon as 'generally dry, methodical, and un-affecting; delivered with the most insipid calmness'. On the other hand, after 1660 a plain style was cultivated, reflecting a need to get the Christian message over to the laity. In the diocese of Canterbury a cleric wrote that his 'church is generally full where there is a sermon, but scandalously thin when there is none. The houses stand at a distance from the church and the people all resort to neighbouring churches, as they say, for the sake of hearing a sermon.'

The Interregnum had also taken its toll on communion. However much the clergy in the Church of England wanted more numerous celebrations, it rarely occurred except on what became known as the four Sacrament Sundays, which were chosen from Christmas, Easter, Whitsun, Palm Sunday and Michaelmas. Although some churches cele-brated communion more often, the legacy of the reign of Puritanism had been to engender a general reluctance to receive the sacrament. In Wiltshire even the norm of four was not met, virtually all churches having only one annual celebration – some of them at Christmas rather than Easter, which was supposedly mandatory – and some did not even achieve that. James Garth, the cleric of Halperton in the same county from 1673 to 1702, had some 200 parishioners but only 14 communicants. Thomas Secker, archbishop of Canterbury from 1758 to 1768, wrote: 'Some imagine that the sacrament belongs only to persons of advanced years, or great leisure, and it is a very dangerous thing for common persons to venture on.' This reluctance was partly an inheritance from the Interregnum years, when the minister had selected those he deemed worthy to receive communion. It was also fuelled by the threatening admonition that had to be read from the Prayer Book on the Sunday before communion was celebrated: without penitence and reconciliation, 'the receiving of the Holy Communion doth nothing else but increase your damnation'. The alternative address, which was rarely used, was also hardly encouraging and again spelled out that, if received unworthily, 'we eat and drink to our damnation'. All of this caused a general fear of receiving communion; it also explains the practice of partaking only when older because there was less likelihood of reoffending.

In stark contrast, the rites of passage administered by the Anglican Church remained important. Confirmation became extremely popular as superstition held that it was a cure for rheumatism; consequently many put themselves forward to be confirmed more than once. The 1753 Marriage Act, which outlawed clandestine marriages – held in secret without the calling of the banns – laid down that only unions solemnised by the Church of England were legally binding so that Catholics, for example, were forced to have two weddings; those who could not afford the expense had to make do with the Anglican rite only.

Catechism was still supposed to take place each Sunday after the second lesson at Evening Prayer but it was never popular. It was first neglected and then gradually abandoned, its role eventually taken over by charity-school instruction. Self-examination replaced auricular confession, although voluntary confession continued as provided for in the Book of Common Prayer. Public penance for breaking the moral code still occurred, but as the century progressed, such acts migrated to the privacy of the parsonage. Fees for burials, a major source of income for the clergy, were deeply resented, but it is extraordinary that not only Anglicans were buried in the churchyard but also Dissenters and Catholics, who could be interred at night – as long as they had paid the fees. In theory burial could not be denied but ministers were quite capable of holding families to ransom. With the Restoration came a return to the formality of the Prayer Book ritual: the body, covered with a hearse cloth, was carried in procession to the churchyard gate where it was met by the minister who performed the ritual. Only Quakers were buried elsewhere as they refused to recognise any ceremony or the concept of consecrated ground.

Finally, I must write about the greatest change affecting the parish church: the return of music. As we have seen, after the Reformation music and singing became the province of the chapels royal and the cathedrals; only psalm singing was a feature of parish worship – and it was viewed as tainted by Puritanism. Psalm singing had been accorded a full place for the first time in the *Directory of Public Worship* of 1645: 'it is the duty of Christians to praise God publicly, by singing of psalms together in the congregation, and also privately in the family'. After 1660 psalm singing was incorporated into Anglican parish worship but in the repetitive form known as 'lining-out'. That practice had been described in the *Directory*: 'where many of the congregation cannot read, it is convenient that the minister, or some other fit person appointed by him and the other ruling officers, do read the psalm, line by line, before the singing thereof'. The musician Thomas Mace lamented in his *Musick's Monument* (1676) that it was 'sad to hear what whining, toting, yelling, or screeching there is in many country congregations'. The practice of 'lining-out' was slow, ponderous and drawn out, wrecking any poetic or musical quality that the singing might have had – although this was not to impede its popularity with congregations.

Attempts to change 'the old way of singing' proved an uphill task. Parishioners stuck to the tunes they knew, essentially those published by Sternhold and Hopkins in 1562. Tate and Brady's up-to-date settings published in 1696 defeated them, although they ran to 295 editions. In 1700 the Lacock parish vestry-meeting in Wiltshire decided 'that the old tunes to the psalms of David which have always heretofore been used and sung in the said parish church . . . be continued. And that noe other new tunes be sung there for the future.' Change was achieved more easily in the towns by the introduction of an organ, but even if a country church could afford one no one could play it.

In 1686, an anonymous publication entitled *A new and easie method to learn to sing by book* provided the earliest adumbration of a parish church choir: 'It would therefore be a commendable thing if six, eight or more sober young men that have good voices, would associate and form themselves into a choir . . . a few such in a congregation . . . might in a little time bring into the church better singing than is common, and more variety of good tunes.' Even though this idea was advocated by the SPCK and other religious societies, it needed the support of the incumbent who all too often saw such a suggestion as amounting to the introduction of popery.

Such choirs called for singing teachers – in the main they came from London – who toured the regions training the parish clerks who in their turn instructed the singers. In order to achieve the right pitch pipes were used, but by the middle of the eighteenth century instruments began to appear in the form of the cello or bassoon. After 1770 village bands also made their appearance. The players and singers either stood together in a particular pew or were accommodated in what was a musician's gallery at the west end of the church. Parson Woodforde described the arrival of singers in his diary entry for 9 September 1792: 'Weston singers sang this Afternoon and very well.' Singers also visited on 23 February 1794: 'Mattishall Singers were at Church and sung exceedingly well, attended with a bass-viol and an Hautboy . . .'

A village choir, late eighteenth century. The men and youths sing from a single book, the leader holding a pitch-pipe.

Inevitably choirs became more ambitious wanting to sing ever more elaborate anthems. The larger their role in the liturgy, however, the more they were resented by the congregations whose psalm singing gradually lost its place in the service. Nonetheless the choirs were extremely popular with those who sang, a motley array of shopkeepers, landowners and domestics taking part in a community activity that came to be seen as the peak of village life. But the advent of choirs was also not welcomed by many clerics. The bishop of Salisbury, Thomas Sherlock, for instance, warned against persons meeting 'at unseasonable times under pretence of learning to sing psalms . . .' and in the 1720s started a campaign to suppress the choirs in his diocese; in the previous decade they had also been suppressed in Exeter. Thus not every part of the country took part in this musical revival, but it was hugely popular in the West Riding of Yorkshire, South Lancashire, the North Midlands, East Anglia and the South-west.

In addition, by the close of the eighteenth century hymns made their appearance in the Church of England. They had originated with the Methodists, and the great hymn writers Charles Wesley and Isaac Watts, but they gradually percolated into the parish churches. When in 1820 their use was challenged in the Consistory Court of York, it declared in their favour, precipitating the flood of hymnals so typical of the Victorian age. These hymns added emotional spirituality to an arid liturgy: they spoke of penitence and conversion, of pardon, and of the sanctification of ordinary life. They were embraced above all by the evangelical revival within the Church of England at the end of the eighteenth century, and the most important collection was the *Olney Hymns* (1779). Like psalm singing in the past, hymns provided the ordinary worshipper with an active role to play during the service.

As in previous centuries, we know very little of what the man in the pew thought of all this. Certainly attendance at the parish church was regarded more than ever as an expression of patriotism in an age that saw Britain perpetually at war with continental Catholic powers.

As the parishioners sat in church, their eyes were fixed on the pulpit and reading desk, and their ears tuned in to the Prayer Book liturgy and readings from the Authorised Version of the Bible. There is a comforting absence of turbulence about the Church in Georgian England, but it would prove to be the calm before the storm that was to change the face of virtually every country church. In the opening decades of the nineteenth century it became obvious that the Church of England had become fossilised and too inflexible to respond to the rapidly changing times.

Chapter 8

The Rainbow Comes and Goes

THE CHURCH OF THE HOLY Innocents at Highnam today lies on the outskirts of the conurbation of Gloucester, but when it was built between 1848 and 1851, it provided a church for some 300 people who, up until then, had to make their way to the neighbouring village of Churcham. Everything about this church is amazing – from its astonishing steeple, which can be seen for miles around, to the jewel box of an interior. Compared to Mildenhall, altered only thirty years before, Highnam comes as a cultural shock: here we see the attempt to put the clock back to fourteenth-century England – as though the Reformation had never happened. Unbelievably, this church was built in the age of the railway and the penny post.

At Highnam, the whole design of the church focuses on the altar, which can be glimpsed through a screen and is approached by steps. On the altar itself we see candlesticks and a cross, and behind it arises an elaborately carved reredos. Every surface in the church is smothered with decoration – sculpted, painted or stencilled; even the radiators have pitched roofs like medieval reliquaries. Above the chancel arch Christ is shown enthroned in majesty, flanked by the Apostles and attended by flights of trumpeting angels in shades of pink, pistachio, blue and gold. The walls and arches are covered with spiralling leaves and flowers embowering sacred monograms. The windows are filled with stained glass filtering the light into pools of colour. While Mildenhall exuded the light and clarity of the age of Enlightenment, everything at Highnam seems to be about reverence and the celebration of the holy mysteries at the altar. It is an astonishing change of atmosphere.

I visited Highnam on a brilliant autumn day, its bold Gothic silhouette clear-cut against a blue sky. The church is part of a whole complex and nearby I could glimpse the rectory and the sacristan's lodge and also, in the distance, across the parkland, the great house itself, Highnam Court. Holy Innocents is an estate church built at enormous expense by a wealthy aesthete, Thomas Gambier Parry. Both his father and grandfather had been directors of the East India Company and Gambier Parry purchased the estate at the age of twenty-one. The church was later erected in memory of his first wife, Isabella, the dedication reflecting the loss of four of their five children. It was consecrated on 29 April 1851 with great celebrations and when all the guests had departed, the solitary figure of Gambier Parry himself was seen carrying the bust of his wife into the church to place it in the niche of a side chapel. There it has stood to this day.

It is rare to find a church where so much converges in a single building. Thomas Gambier Parry was a founder-member of the Cambridge Camden Society in 1839, whose mission it was to return English churches to the golden age of the fourteenth century. For Highnam Gambier Parry employed Henry Woodyer, a pupil of the eminent architect William Butterfield, whose most famous church, All Saints, Margaret Street, London, epitomised the ideals of the Anglican spiritual revival we know as that of Anglo-Catholicism. Holy Innocents is its equivalent in a rural setting. It is a monument to a section of the Church of England that wished to put the clock back and which, in a sense, tried to wipe out the Reformation. This attempt was as revolutionary as the iconoclasm that had destroyed the church interiors three centuries before. There was, however, a difference: in the sixteenth century the Reformation was imposed from on high; in the nineteenth the changes were pioneered by a group of reforming clerics and laymen who formed what we know as the Oxford Movement.

In 1800 the Church of England was still the nation's most powerful religious and cultural institution. Its head was the king, its bishops were landed aristocrats who sat in the Lords, and many of its clergy were

Holy Innocents, Highnam, Gloucestershire.

drawn from the ranks of the aristocracy and gentry. The Church also retained the monopoly of public office and of access to Oxford and Cambridge. But despite its powerful position, at the turn of the century it became obvious that the Church was heading towards crisis. During the last decades of the eighteenth century, many of its flock had turned to Methodism or become Baptists and Congregationalists. Methodism in particular had a huge appeal with its concern for personal salvation and its stress on the equality of sinners, regardless of social status. This stood in sharp contrast to the Church of England's cold formalism and its role as the guarantor of social hierarchy and deference; if you were religious during this period you would almost certainly have been a Methodist. At the turn of the century, an evangelical revival took place within the Church of England itself, led by the likes of William Wilberforce and the Clapham Sect, which drew a section of the upper classes back to a life of personal piety and dedication to social and moral causes. But its inspirations and energies came mostly from without the Church and not from within, and it was thus viewed by many Anglican clerics as smacking of the 'enthusiasm' of Dissenters and Methodists.

By the 1820s the crisis of the Church was there for everyone to see. Attacks were mounted on its corruption, nepotism, sinecures and other financial abuses. The Dissenters now rose in protest bitterly resenting the fact that they had to pay the church rate to maintain what was not their church, and as a result, the Test and Corporation Act abolished legal penalties for Dissenters in 1828. The following year saw the Catholic Emancipation Act, which marked the end of the Church of England's monopoly of public office and the universities. These erosions of Anglican exclusivity continued unabated through the century. In 1836, for example, Dissenters were allowed to marry in their own chapels or before a registrar, and in 1850 they gained admission to the universities. If the Church of England felt beleaguered by Dissent, it felt equally threatened by Roman Catholicism. The numbers of Catholics in England were boosted by Irish immigrants, and in 1850 came the shock of a restored hierarchy, when the Church of England was faced with a parallel Roman Catholic episcopate and parish system. Fear of Rome, bred out of centuries of being a beleaguered Protestant island at war with the Catholic powers of Europe, resurfaced.

All of this forced the Church of England to reflect on its identity and its place in society. In 1833, in his famous 'Sermon on National Apostasy', John Keble threw down the gauntlet to Parliament, which was proposing to suppress ten Irish bishoprics, daring it to intervene in the affairs of an institution which was both catholic and divine. His speech marked the beginning of the Oxford Movement, which sought to restore the High Church ideals of the Laudian divines with a renewed emphasis both on the apostolic succession of the Anglican clergy and on the Church as a divine institution through its ministry of the sacraments. Its leaders were men of outstanding intellectual calibre. They included John Keble (1792–1866), a distinguished poet and author of *The Christian Year* (1827); Edward Bouverie Pusey (1800–92), a patristic scholar who was to be instrumental in the revival of monastic life in the Church of England; and the most brilliant of all, John Henry Newman (1801–90). The movement was to receive a major blow in 1845 when Newman was received into the Roman Catholic Church, where he would become a cardinal, but the influence of his writings on the Church of England cannot be overestimated. The *Tracts for the Times* (1833–41), launched by these men, caused a sensation, drawing upon the Early Church Fathers together with the works of the Jacobean and Caroline divines in order to reawaken the slumbering sacramental life of the Church, to reassert its catholicity, to uphold the sacred nature of the priesthood and to place at the centre a revitalised liturgy. The Oxford Movement stressed the importance of tradition and corporate holiness, a position diametrically opposed to the evangelical wing of the Church with its focus on Scripture and personal salvation.

No part of the Church of England was to remain untouched by the Oxford Movement. Its early exponents and followers were labelled

Tractarians, and its more advanced party became known as Anglo-Catholics. But the movement was divisive. Its theological stance, although deeply rooted in the works of the Church Fathers and the Anglican divines of the seventeenth century, came to be viewed as taking the Church back to Rome. It led to the reordering of churches, the introduction of greater formality in worship, and the return of vestments, ceremonial and images. These reforms later led to a series of court cases as the Low Church wing attempted to curtail what they viewed as the introduction of popery. But in the long run no one could stop or control what went on in the parishes, and the Oxford Movement would soon affect the ordinary country church, even if often only in a minor way. It led to changes to its interior and the conduct of the liturgy that were more radical than anything that had occurred since the Reformation.

This departure ran parallel with another development that would change the countryside for ever: the agrarian and industrial revolutions. In 1801 about 20 per cent of the population lived in cities or towns; a century later 75 per cent was urban. The agrarian revolution was already well under way by the close of the eighteenth century, pioneered by landowners who enclosed the fields and introduced new farming techniques, irrevocably changing the nature of rural society. Traditional work patterns and social relationships that had been founded on rank and custom were replaced with contractual wage labour, which soon created a rural proletariat.

For centuries the village had been defined by the ownership of land that was widely, if unevenly, distributed. Although there were huge inequalities in terms of wealth, status and power, everyone shared the land; even families that had no stake in it had access to common land and common rights over open fields. In the nineteenth century the old rural society was gradually reconfigured into three quite distinct classes: landowners, tenant farmers and landless labourers. Divisions sharpened as both landowners and farmers, in response to an increasing sense of social hierarchy and class status, withdrew from the communal life of the village. The landowner, who often held the advowson, continued to regard the parish church virtually as his own property, controlling the choice of incumbent and influencing what went on inside.

If the nature of rural society changed, so did the parish. In 1800 it was still the principal agency of local government. The vestry, chaired by the incumbent and consisting of the major ratepayers, was responsible for poor relief, apprenticeship schemes, schools, roads, public health and, by way of the parish constable, policing. The vestry also maintained the church and was entitled to raise money for its upkeep from the parishioners. By 1900 all these responsibilities, except caring for the church building, had been taken away by the Local Government Act of 1894. As central legislation was imposed, the village ceased to be isolated. In addition, first the railways and later the motorcar invaded and opened it up to the outside world. National newspapers and other cheap printed matter now penetrated even the remotest hamlet, breaking down traditional, inward-looking communities.

A parish vestry meeting, late eighteenth century.

It is extraordinary that the old medieval parish and its church survived the social changes of the nineteenth century. The survival of the parish flew in the face of Victorian urbanisation, yet it lived on only as an ecclesiastical unit, for in every other sense the old world had vanished. The size of country parishes could still vary wildly. In the West Midlands and in Cornwall parishes ranged in size from 3,000 to 6,000 acres, while in the north and west some were larger than 10,000 acres. There existed two types of parish, 'open' and 'closed'. In the 'closed' parish the control lay in the hands of an alliance between the squire and the parson; together with a group of the major farmers they could form a 'ring'. In 'open' parishes control was more scattered, in the absence of a major landowner or resident cleric. The Church of England of course favoured 'closed' parishes, where the village church was still a monument to deference and hierarchy under the paternalistic rule of squire and parson, the old alliance of the great house and the rectory.

Although nothing was done to update the parish system to reflect the demographic shifts of the century, there was a sustained drive to eradicate non-residence, to bring an end to clerics who lived in town during the week and only rode out to their parish on Sunday. In addition, in 1829 a Commission of Inquiry into the Ecclesiastical Revenues of England and Wales was set up, the first since 1524. Its findings led to the Pluralities Act of 1838, which laid down that no cleric could hold more than two benefices, that they should not be more than ten miles apart and that their joint value was not to exceed £1,000 per year. In 1850 the distance was narrowed down to three miles and the income of one of the benefices was not to exceed £100 per annum. A major problem, however, was the absence of a parsonage in many villages. A survey in 1835 recorded 1,728 parsonages as being unfit for habitation and 2,878 parishes as having no parsonage at all. Thanks to the agricultural boom in the middle decades of the nineteenth century, all over England rectories and vicarages now arose on a large scale – houses with suites of rooms for entertaining, several bedrooms, servants' quarters and stables. At Bemerton, near Salisbury, the modest rectory that had once housed George Herbert was extended to accommodate the rector, his wife, four daughters, ten indoor servants, two gardeners and two stablemen. By 1878 the rectory at Long Melford in Suffolk had five reception rooms, sixteen bedrooms and three dressing rooms. In the Victorian age, some clergy finally achieved their dream of becoming gentlemen, riding out to the hounds, playing cards and cricket, and gardening.

There were more in holy orders in the nineteenth century than at any time since the Middle Ages: between 1830 and 1875 the number of parishes with a resident cleric doubled, and between 1841 and 1911 the number of clergy overall rose from 14,613 to 24,968. (The nineteenth century's obsession with statistics enables us for the first time to gain a comprehensive picture of the changes that occurred.) Once appointed, however, they were immovable until death, and some parishes could be stuck with the same incumbent for up to half a century. One can appreciate the attraction of the Methodist congregations who changed their ministers every three years. The clergy's finances now began to improve. In 1835 a report found that the typical annual income of an incumbent was £275, while earnings of £395 were viewed as desirable. But even this income set the clergy apart as belonging to the top 10 to 15 per cent of the national average. It continued to come from various sources, such as fees for weddings, churchings and burials as well as what could be earned from teaching. The tithe, in cash or in kind, was finally abolished in 1868 in favour of a voluntary contribution. The glebe land remained and could vary in size from as little as nine acres in the diocese of Rochester to more than thirty in that of Oxford. But the agricultural depression of the 1870s would reduce the cleric's income by a third, thus making holy orders no longer an attractive proposition for younger sons of the gentry. Gradually the clergy ceased to be an extension of the established classes.

By then the very nature of the clerical profession had changed too. As we have seen, at the opening of the century clerics only had a classical education. It was in the middle decades of the nineteenth century that special preparation for the ministry was introduced with the founding of training colleges at Chichester (1840), Wells (1840) and Cuddesdon (1854). But it was not until the 1880s that such training became the norm, and it was finally institutionalised in 1912 when the Central Advisory Council of Training for the Ministry was set up. This recasting of the clerical role went hand in hand with the recovery of pastoral ministry of a kind rarely exercised in the eighteenth century. The country clergy became active in all kinds of reforming social endeavours, founding and supporting village schools, creating benefit and provident clubs to aid the poor of the parish or giving them allotments on the glebe land.

It is ironic that the Victorian era is still viewed as the great age of churchgoing; in fact, the statistics demonstrate that the reverse was true. The 1851 census revealed that the vast mass of the population never attended church; those who did came from the upper and middle classes. The increase in the number of communicants at Easter from 1,110,000 in 1831 to 2,293,000 in 1911 did not reflect the overall population growth from 13,900,000 to 36,000,000 over the same period. The Church never won over the working classes in town and country: the clergy was regarded as an arm of the ruling elite. The agrarian labourers never forgave them for their part in suppressing the rural disturbances of 1830–2, known as the Swing riots, nor, later in the century, for joining with the landowners in the suppression of unions.

In spite of this, the nineteenth century experienced a boom in church building in the countryside, often served by architects of the highest calibre including Butterfield, A. W. Blomfield, G. E. Street, Ewan Christian and G. F. Bodley. Many were built – and many more rebuilt or restored. In the diocese of Rochester, for instance, all 130 churches were restored between 1840 and 1880, in South Lindsey in Lincolnshire major work was carried out on 127 churches between 1840

Turning the clock back: Bicknor Church, Kent, as it was in 1858 and as it would be after G. F. Bodley's restoration.

and 1875, and in England as a whole some 7,000 churches were restored. Unlike the building boom in the Middle Ages, this was not a grass-roots expression of rural spirituality; on the contrary, it could be described as an aspect of estate management during the agricultural golden age between 1850 and 1875. Ironically, many newly built or restored churches deliberately set out to recreate the pre-capitalist medieval world. Yet although one of the arguments for demolishing the old box pews was that they embodied private property and social exclusiveness, the new pews served to seat the congregation according to the class system of capitalist agriculture with landowners at the front and labourers (if they ever came) at the back. Paradoxically, the new pews created more space for the congregation – between 20 and 50 per cent more worshippers could be accommodated in the new arrangement – during a period when church attendance and thus demand for seating was in radical decline.

*　　*　　*

What these new and restored churches looked like and what happened inside them was largely conditioned by a single publication. In 1839 Dr John Mason Neale and Benjamin Webb founded the Cambridge Camden (later Ecclesiological) Society, followed two years later by a journal, the *Ecclesiologist*. Nothing like this had existed in the Church of England before: a regular publication dedicated exclusively to church architecture, decoration and liturgy. Its aim was 'to promote the study of Ecclesiastical Architecture and the restoration of mutilated architectural remains'. In the wake of the celebrated architect, A. W. Pugin, Gothic architecture was designated as the only true Christian style and the Decorated period of the fourteenth century in particular was deemed most perfect. One of the earliest Victorian rural churches to be affected by the Society was Kilndown in Kent. Between 1840 and 1845, the lord of the manor, Alexander James Beresford Hope, transformed its chancel into an elaborately decorated altar area reflecting the Oxford Movement's desire that a church interior should proclaim a Church that was catholic, sacerdotal and sacramental. The ecclesiological movement captured the imagination of a younger generation that was in the throes of Romanticism and its fascination with the medieval world.

In their local parish church, rich aristocrats would put into practice what they had read in the *Ecclesiologist*. In that publication Georgian churches were denounced as preaching boxes: triple-decker pulpits and box pews should be thrown out. Church interiors had to be rearranged according to catholic principles, and the focus now shifted from the pulpit to the chancel, its screen, and beyond that the altar with a stepped approach. New churches had to be built in the Decorated style and, whenever possible, old ones had that style imposed upon them. As one country vicar wrote in the 1850s: 'The Church was strangely altered, "restored" to an appearance which it had certainly never possessed before. Out from it went the box pews, and the old three-decker; and out alas! Went Norman arches as well as giving place to Gothick reproductions in the middle period.'

The drive to make manifest the continuation of the Anglican

Church with the pre-Reformation Catholic Church led to a wholesale return of symbolism and imagery. A whole industry sprang up of church furnishers and decorators – the firm of Morris & Co. being the most notable – capable of painting and stencilling walls, supplying stained glass, statues, crosses, candlesticks, lecterns, vestments, altar frontals and banners. This was the return of images on a massive scale,

Stained glass window by Sir Edward Burne-Jones, St Margaret, Rottingdean, East Sussex, *c.* 1890.

The church interior before . . .

all aimed at creating an atmosphere of mysterious beauty, reverence
and wonder. In addition, comforts such as heating arrived by the middle
of the century as well as oil lamps, then gas, and finally electric light.
The latter made evening services possible for the first time.

Members of the ecclesiological movement travelled the country
recording the state of parish churches. The *Ecclesiologist* reported in
1842 with horror that of churches in Cambridgeshire. The chancel at
Longstanton in Cambridgeshire was used as a school with a curtain
drawn across the chancel arch, and in the north wall a 'common kitchen
fire-grate' had been inserted. At Little Shelford the chancel was filled
with deal forms and straw mats, the Holy Table 'a wretched deal frame,
painted red', and at Hardwick it was a 'rude frame of rough pieces of
deal hammered together and painted red. It was covered with a dirty
and torn rag of the very coarsest green baize.' Suddenly all over the
country people were horrified at the state of church interiors.

. . . and after reordering, 1868.

The transformation that often followed – depending on the commitment and views of the local landowner and the cleric – must have come as an enormous shock to many congregations: where previously there had been a whitewashed shell filled with family pews and a three-decker pulpit obscuring the chancel, there now arrived pews in serried ranks facing an altar adorned with a cross, candlesticks and brass vases filled with flowers. One by one the windows would be filled with newly commissioned stained glass and the altar would be vested with the changing colours of the liturgical seasons. There are few churches today whose interior wasn't radically altered during the Victorian period.

The Oxford Movement also precipitated a liturgical revival. The Elizabethan Settlement had stipulated that the interiors of churches should be left as they were in 1549, before the purges of the iconoclasts. It took the Oxford Movement little antiquarian research to establish that at that time the churches were still fully furnished in the late medieval manner and that vestments, holy water and incense were all still in use. The quest to reinstate the Church of England's newly found catholicity not only visually but also liturgically began with William Maskell's *The Ancient Liturgy of the Church of England* (1844) and *Monumenta Ritualia Ecclesiae Anglicanae* (1846), and culminated in 1858 with the publication of John Purchas's *Directorium Anglicanum* which, although ostensibly working from the 1549 Prayer Book, derived most of its liturgy from the Roman rite. What these books reintroduced into the Church of England can be illustrated by the charges brought against Purchas in 1869 for breaking ecclesiastical law in his capacity as perpetual curate of St James's Chapel in Brighton. Among other things he was charged with wearing a cope other than at Holy Communion, sporting a biretta, using wafer bread, mixing water with the wine, placing a crucifix and candles on the altar, using holy water, facing east at the altar, introducing images, using incense and staging processions. Purchas's book was to remain the standard liturgical authority for many decades, although by the 1920s Percy Dearmer's *The Parson's Handbook* (1899), which went through many editions, had become the norm of liturgical practice in a wide range of parish churches touched by the ideals of the Oxford Movement.

Despite this burrowing into the medieval past, the reforms hardly recreated what had happened in church during the Middle Ages. One difference, for example, was the arrival of the surpliced choir. Although some church choirs had worn cassocks and surplices in the past, the defining deployment of this new phenomenon can be seen in the parish church in Leeds, consecrated in 1841, the first to be built directly in response to the dictates of the Cambridge Camden Society. The band and the singers in the west gallery vanished, and a fully robed choir was sited in stalls between the congregation and the sanctuary. This introduced to the parish church an arrangement that could previously be found only in cathedrals. With it came the arrival of another fixture: the organ. After some hesitation the Cambridge Camden Society had agreed to an organ being placed to the

The entry of the clergy as envisaged in the 1932 edition of Percy Dearmer's *The Parson's Handbook*.

north or south side of the chancel. Where it was introduced into country churches with a narrow chancel, the effect was catastrophic. Moreover, its arrival was not always welcomed with open arms, for it made village musicians and parish clerks redundant. Banished from the church, the village musicians found refuge outside in the pubs and taverns, for example in Yorkshire, where the old folk carols are still sung with vigour to this day.

This new arrangement reduced the congregation to the role of onlookers who glimpsed the theatrical spectacle through the screen. Moreover, the move by the High Church Anglicans to introduce more elaborate ritual into the performance of the liturgy ended the uniformity that had existed, more or less, since 1662. We now witness a huge discrepancy in atmosphere between Low and High Church services: at one end we find the bare, whitewashed preaching houses of the evangelicals, with a table for an altar and the incumbent in a surplice; in other churches the Prayer Book communion service was made to resemble the late medieval Mass with the celebrant facing eastwards, mixing water with the wine in the chalice, using wafers rather than bread, elevating the Host and chalice to the tinkling of a sacring bell, and using incense. But few churches went that far. Even in 1900 in only 10 per cent of churches were vestments worn, incense used or would statues of saints with votive candles be present. And in the main, they would be urban churches, especially those in poor areas. In most churches, particularly in the countryside, Holy Communion continued to be celebrated as it had been in the previous century. In the second half of the nineteenth century people began to speak of the 'Broad Church', situated somewhere in the middle between the extremes, which accepted the surpliced choir and the placing of cross and candlesticks on the altar but stopped short at vestments and incense. In this way few parish churches remained unaffected in appearance and ritual by this major revival of liturgical studies.

Throughout the nineteenth century we witness a move towards making communion the main Sunday service. The term 'Eucharist' also began to be used, avoiding both the Low Church's 'Lord Supper' with its commemorative connotations and the High Church's 'Mass' with its suggestion of sacrifice and offering. Change was slow and the old sequence of Morning Prayer, litany, sermon and ante-communion remained in place in many churches, but as the century progressed, it became apparent that in an ever-faster-moving world this Sunday sequence was increasingly anomalous. In 1872 the Act of Uniformity Amendment Act allowed clergy to adapt services and, for the first time, to separate Morning Prayer, litany and Holy Communion. The act laid the foundations for our services today, and by 1900 had created a pattern of Sunday worship with communion at 8 a.m., followed by Morning Prayer as the principal service.

Sermons remained important in a turbulent era during which the biblical truths were challenged by the discoveries of geology and

Darwinism, much to the bewilderment of many believers. But sermons now rarely lasted longer than twenty or thirty minutes. Here too there was a strong division between High and Low Church. The evangelicals dwelled on the redeeming merits of Christ's blood, justification by faith alone and the centrality of personal conversion, while Anglo-Catholics spoke of the saints, the sacraments and the Church as the mystical Body of Christ. Most clerics now wrote their own sermons, although handbooks like the Reverend J. G. Pilkington's *The Spiritual Garland* went through nine editions by 1882, and Arthur Roberts, the rector of Woodrising in Norfolk for fifty-five years, produced no less than seventeen volumes of village sermons.

There can be no doubt but that churchgoing changed far more radically during the Victorian period than at any other time since the mid-seventeenth century. Services looked and sounded different. The music of the cathedral by composers such as Thomas Tallis and William Byrd, along with a revival of Gregorian chant, now made their way into the parish church. Hymns, once regarded as tainted by Methodism by the old High Church, were now incorporated into the Anglican canon and taken up by Reginald Heber (1783–1826), rector of Hodnet and later Bishop of Calcutta. Heber wrote popular hymns like 'Holy, holy, holy', which were sung at Morning Prayer before the sermon. The Oxford Movement had also discovered a wealth of them in the Roman breviary, and although they had not been translated by Thomas Cranmer, they were seen as belonging to the orbit of the Book of Common Prayer. Among the numerous hymn books two were to outshine all others – *Hymns Ancient and Modern* (1860–1) and *The English Hymnal* (1906). In revised form, both are still in use today.

We catch this gradual transformation in the records of seventeen parishes in rural Sussex. In 1853 ten of them had no music at all. One possessed an organ, two had finger organs, two responded to a flute and one to a pitch-pipe. Eight years later psalms were chanted in nine of them, and in five *Hymns Ancient and Modern* were used. But the arrival of the barrel organ, the harmonium and the pipe organ made the old village orchestra and singers led by the parish clerk redundant and along with them extinguished a certain kind of communal exuberance in worship.

Clerical diaries shed light on what went on at ground level during this time. Born in 1808, Richard Seymour came from a distinguished naval and clerical family and was the son of a baronet. He started out as an evangelical but was later strongly influenced by the Oxford Movement. In 1834 he was appointed to the rectory of Kinwarton with Alne in Warwickshire. Seymour was a typical example of an upper-class Victorian country cleric who had married into a county family, took long holidays on the continent, lived in a large rectory with several servants, gave dinner parties and indulged in cricket and archery. But he was also a reforming cleric.

His diary entry for 12 October 1834 catches what it was like in church before the ecclesiological reforms: 'Morning Service at Kinwarton; not very encouraging congregation. Eight in all. Afternoon Service Great Alne. More in number, but the children noisy. The appearance of the Church very sad. Hope to effect a change in the edifice and the people.' Seymour was a man of action and three years later the restoration began. In 1837 he celebrated the Eucharist with thirty-nine communicants; from 1839 communion was celebrated monthly, and in addition Seymour introduced prayers on Ash Wednesday and during Holy Week. This went hand in hand with opening village schools and starting evening classes for adult villagers. In 1842 he introduced services for all the great festivals of the Church year and on Ember days. In 1844 communion was celebrated on Maundy Thursday for the first time: 'at last kept the day in a proper way', Seymour recorded. Two years later he extended the Lenten fast to his servants.

In 1847 William Butterfield, the architect of All Saints in Margaret Street, came to advise Seymour on the church roof. As Butterfield was at the heart of the ecclesiological movement it is hardly surprising that when Kinwarton church reopened not only had the box pews gone but oil lamps had arrived along with a new service book. Seymour's diary records the changes that took place in many parishes at the time. An harmonium was installed in the chancel in 1852, and a choir was formed at Great Alne in 1855. In 1860, the church reopened again after further 'enlargement and improvement'. Five years later Easter decorations are mentioned for the first time, and Seymour took part in a communion service at Norwich staged like a Roman Catholic High Mass with the clergy in vestments and the attendance of acolytes, all 'robed as abroad. It was a strange sight, but the service was very solemn.'

All of these changes challenged congregations who were resistant to change. At first it was difficult to get parishioners to join in the singing but it gradually caught on, giving the public a new kind of folk religion

The vanishing village choir, *c.* 1853.

which lives on today. But some parishioners objected to the choir and the organ, the latter's sonorous and decorous tone contrasting sharply with the noise made by the old village band. Parishioners were often alienated, as caught by Thomas Hardy in his novel *Under the Greenwood Tree*. But what happened during that time was a reformulation of Anglican worship creating the form we still largely know today.

This was the age of the Harvest Festival, which became hugely popular from the 1870s – in the main because it was not a religious festival at all. On the day there would be a procession through the village to church, and after Morning Prayer, in some cases Holy Communion, a collection would be taken for the poor. There followed a dinner provided by the local landowner and farmers, which was rounded off by singing 'God Save the Queen'.

Confirmation was another occasion for feasting; sometimes people would choose to be confirmed two or three times just because of the party that followed and, in the end, multiple confirmations were suppressed. But for many, confirmation marked the end of a person's religious life. Catechising the young and instruction in the faith had migrated to the day and Sunday schools, and the Church of England totally failed to reach down the social spectrum: labourers, dairymaids and farm servants were beyond the reach of the Church. Their world continued to be one of superstition and folklore, as it had been for centuries. In cases where the master insisted that his servants attend church they had to sit in a separate section because their master and mistress were 'too high to associate with them'.

But the parish church still retained its hold on the rites of passage. Marriage continued to be witnessed by the local community, and burial too was a corporate action demanding that the coffin bearers should be of the same status as the deceased. Those of elevated status were carried shoulder high, the rest 'underhand'. The only change came in the 1880 Burial Act which permitted non-Anglicans to use their own rite.

* * *

Christening Sunday, 1887.

Let me close with a final cameo of a country cleric. The Reverend Edward Boys Ellman became rector of Berwick in Sussex at the age of twenty-three in 1844 and was to remain in this parish until 1906. His memoirs, written in anecdotal style, capture the many changes that took place during the second half of the nineteenth century. His daughter wrote that 'there is little doubt but that he was much influenced by the Oxford Movement, and that if he had been in a larger or in a town parish, he would have been willing to have had a more elaborate service. But he thought extremes not acceptable or suited to his people . . .' And that, I think, must have been the attitude that prevailed in many country churches in the Victorian age.

'When I was first ordained,' wrote Ellman, 'anything like church decoration was dreaded; the cross or even the candlesticks on the altar were looked upon as Popish. Flowers were considered the same. The only decoration ever indulged in was at Christmas.' He recalled how services were 'very slovenly taken', and 'Anything in the shape or form of ceremony was avoided as much as possible, and regarded as "Popish". The services were long, the sermons very dry, and as a rule above the understanding certainly of the rural working classes . . .'

Ellman's memoirs record how all of this gradually changed. When Berwick church was reopened after restoration at Easter in 1857, it was, for the first time, decorated with flowers. Soon floral displays appeared at Ascensiontide and Whitsun and later there were flowers on the altar every Sunday. Ellman described how, when he arrived at Berwick, a farmer led the singers with a flute, and a violin was added later. Then, in 1862, a harmonium was bought and in 1880, an organ. In 1870 the congregation was introduced to *Hymns Ancient and Modern*. In these homespun memoirs we catch the ripple effects on a single country parish of the Oxford Movement as recorded by a man who had heard John Henry Newman preach in the 1830s.

But Ellman's gentle, somewhat idyllic evocation of Victorian church life in the country masks the reality: that the Church of England had lost its influence over the nation. The thousands of churches that were built or renovated in the nineteenth century seem to testify to a rural spiritual renaissance; in fact, they were monuments to failure. Ordinary country folk viewed the local church as epitomising a world of deference and respectability which they wished to move away from. Certainly they turned to it for rites of passage, but otherwise most existed in a twilight world of popular folklore intertwined with a robust folk Protestantism. The Church of England had failed to embrace the world of superstition, which the medieval Catholic Church had so successfully incorporated with its array of saints, giving meaning to the life cycle of ordinary people in terms they could understand. What replaced it at the Reformation never captured the rural working classes. The parish church was indelibly viewed as an agent of social control ensuring that the existing hierarchy should continue as of right. Alas, by the close of the nineteenth century it had lost its grip, and in the twentieth this social function would disappear altogether. Shorn of its role in local government, blighted by demographic change and increasingly frozen in time after the arrival of the preservation movement, the English country church was heading towards redundancy.

Epilogue

I SHALL END THIS LITTLE history in a personal way. My late wife and I moved to Herefordshire in the spring of 1973, a fact that explains why so many churches in this book are within striking distance of where I live in Much Birch, one of the seven parishes of the so-called Wormelow Hundred, each with its own church. As I write I stare at the cover of the current church newsletter which has a sketch of St Mary and St Thomas à Becket church, Much Birch, as viewed from near St Mary's church, Little Birch. The fact that you can virtually see one parish church from another is evidence of the huge number of churches in this county. And few of them have closed.

There are a priest and an assistant priest in charge to run this empire – reminiscent of the pluralism of the Georgian period but without its financial incentives. In my church newsletter, on the page headed 'Services this Month', there is a bewildering list of Holy Communion, Morning Worship, Family Communion, Matins and Family Worship taking place at each of these churches. For the two clerics each Sunday is a marathon race as they tear from one service to the next. (Who would want such a job?) But the fact that it continues shows the hold that the parish church still has on those around it, even if there is only a handful of worshippers in the pews. As during the Victorian period, the churches, apart from Christmas, are now mostly visited for what in essence are gatherings unrelated to the Christian calendar – Harvest Festival and Remembrance Sunday (prayers for the dead returned widely after the First World War). Out of the seven churches of the Wormelow Hundred, three perhaps might merit preservation as historic monuments, but it would be difficult to defend the continued existence of the others. And yet to propose shutting them down would let loose untold passions.

The first church my wife and I went to was Much Birch, rebuilt in the year of Victoria's accession and a building devoid of distinction. We started going there in the 1970s, a period of experimentation with new forms of service. The 'thees' and 'thous' were still firmly in place, the choir remained in the choir stalls, but the priest now faced the congregation over the altar. When the Peace was given, my wife found her hand seized in a way that dismayed her, having been nourished on girls' public school religion.

Up the road we then went to a tiny tea-cosy of a church, with a unique dedication to St Junabius and a screen rightly designated by Pevsner as 'an extremely pretty piece'. This was a journey back in time, for it was firmly Morning Prayer each Sunday and communion once a month. But even that was regarded as too frequent by the owner of the large house next to the church, who ran it almost as a private chapel. 'Four times a year was good enough for Queen Victoria,' he said. 'That should be good enough for us.' Here we caught the tail end of what religion must have been like for most people in the Victorian rural parish. The owner of the big house was the churchwarden and rang the bell. Once, to his consternation, a woman arrived to take the service. That he saw was never repeated. On another occasion a priest took the candlesticks from the east window sill and placed them on the altar, from which they were seized and put back again with the comment that he wasn't going to have any popery in this church. Once a farmer and his wife ventured into the church and were promptly shown to a pew at the back. They never returned. I need hardly add that only the Authorised Version of the Bible was used and the 1662 Book of Common Prayer. And that's how it was for several years until we couldn't stand it any more.

So off we went to Christ Church, Llanwarne, a large church built in 1864 in anticipation of a congregation that never came. It replaced the medieval church which now lies below as a picturesque ruin. Constructed in the aftermath of the ecclesiological movement it was, of course, built in the Decorated style with a proper sanctuary, altar with steps, choir stalls and organ. The average Sunday attendance, for what bravely attempted to be a sung Eucharist with a choir of two elderly ladies, was between twelve and twenty. I did occasionally suggest that logic would indicate that this was replaced with a spoken communion service with us gathered in the chancel or in the north transept but I got nowhere. It was rare to see anyone below the age of sixty. By then there was no escaping the new form of service – to which I had no personal objection – when *Common Worship* replaced the Book of Common Prayer in 2000.

Readers who live in the country may well have had similar experiences, which is why, after the death of my wife, I started to go to Hereford Cathedral. On Sundays the cathedral is virtually full; it has a fine ministry of welcome, good music, and the liturgy is performed with accessible ceremony. I leave uplifted and not dispirited. In a way, I was returning to the age before the parish church, when the minsters of Anglo-Saxon England serviced large areas. Then the minster sent out priests into the countryside; today we visit it by car.

What I have described indicates the many changes that affected the average parish church in the twentieth century. The Oxford Movement had successfully restored the centrality of the Eucharist, and in the 1930s that was given a further boost by the Parish and People movement which sought to establish Holy Communion as the supreme expression of corporate worship. After 1945 this gained common acceptance, with Morning Prayer and Evensong going into eclipse. The calls for a revision of the 1662 Book of Common Prayer had begun before 1914, but when a revised version was presented in 1928 it was rejected by the House of Commons. In 1965, Parliament permitted the Church of England to determine its own liturgy, and after various periods of experimentation *Common Worship* was issued in 2000, into which the 1662 Prayer Book was subsumed. It introduced into the performance of the liturgy a far greater participation of the laity through reading lessons, leading corporate prayer, taking the elements up to the altar and administering the chalice. The arrival and acceptance of *Common Worship* meant that contemporary language now replaced mid-Tudor English, and lessons were read from modern translations of the Bible. Some regarded this as a break as violent as doing away with the Latin Mass at the Reformation. In the overwhelmingly conservative countryside this introduction of a succession of new forms of service, which called for the reordering of church interiors, caused widespread upheaval. The altar had to be centred so that the celebrant could face the congregation at Holy Communion, either by pulling it forwards at the east end or by repositioning it at the crossing. In earlier times such alterations had simply been dictated by the state, the local landowner or the incumbent, but now almost every church was a listed building and any changes to the internal fabric had to be approved by a variety of ecclesiastical committees and preservation societies.

The twentieth century also saw the Church of England, along with the other denominations, struggle against the overwhelming tide of secularism. It had gone into steep decline from the 1920s, and by 1979 only 11.5 per cent of the population attended a church of some kind on a Sunday. By 2000 that figure had dropped to 7.5 per cent, and by 2006 the weekly attendance at Church of England services had declined to 1,200,000. Neither the reform of the liturgy nor the advent of women priests, first as deacons in 1987 and then as priests a decade later, has done anything so far to turn the tide. In addition, by 2000 a third of those who went to church were over the age of sixty-five – although that must be balanced by the fact that in the late twentieth century people could 'go to church' by listening to the radio or watching television.

In recent decades the gulf seemed to widen between the majority of the population and the Church, which was viewed as wildly out of tune with society over contemporary attitudes to sexual morality and divorce. Moreover, after the 1960s its influence over the young evaporated as it appeared narrow-minded, conservative and hopelessly out of touch. Although the post-war 1944 Education Act had provided for worship in schools, that became increasingly meaningless in the age of multiculturalism and political correctness. Consequently, any knowledge of the Bible or what constituted a church service was progressively eroded. Churches now became buildings the majority didn't visit or even understand. And yet, when surveys were taken, most of those questioned – 64 per cent according to a poll in 2006 – said that they were Christian. If this was indeed the case, they now seemed to receive the faith through the media or the new information technologies in an era in which religion became increasingly privatised. Yet statistics and polls clearly reflected a residual spiritual yearning of some kind.

At the same time, in a development long overdue, the beleaguered Christian community came together through the ecumenical movement. The various denominations, often for the first time, recognised each other, got to know each other, even if that ended with the realisation that they would have to remain apart. The 1960s witnessed an evangelical revival purveying a Bible-based faith, which now, for instance by means of the Alpha Course, has spread through many parishes. The Evangelical Alliance, founded as long ago as 1846, is now more powerful than ever, its focus shifting from a preoccupation with sin and Hell to one centring on Christ's life as a pattern for social action.

The Church of England entered the twenty-first century as sharply divided as it had been so often in earlier times. It was divided over women priests, with some refusing to accept their ministrations and others converting to Roman Catholicism; it was divided over Scripture, with the evangelicals maintaining biblical literalism while the liberals argued that the Bible as the Word of God had to be read in its historical context; and the issue of homosexuality seemed at times set to tear the whole Church apart.

Where does this leave the English country church? To answer that question we need to look at the church in the context of the reinvention of the village, for in that development should reside the salvation of the church building. Since the close of the Victorian period the urban commercial and professional classes have turned against the city and found a new ideal in the countryside: they were attracted by a vision, largely imaginary, of timelessness – of ancient houses and churches set amidst an immemorial landscape. The advent of the motorcar allied to leisure and disposable income resulted in an invasion of the countryside where houses and cottages were bought as rural retreats, and the story of the village in the twentieth century is largely that of its transformation into a dormitory for commuters, the retired or second-home owners. But while in the second half of the twentieth century many villages would progressively lose their doctor, school, garage, pub, shop and post office, the rural parish church remained as some kind of aberration awaiting its fate. If it had been subject to normal commercial pressures, the country church would have been abandoned years ago as unviable. That they are still there is largely due to voluntary local efforts – but how long will that last? We delude ourselves if we think that interest in preserving country churches extends beyond a tiny minority. Moreover, it is one thing for a wider public to see these churches through a haze of crinoline ladies making their way to them through snow on a Christmas card and quite another to ask the same people to put their hands in their pockets to contribute to their upkeep.

The twentieth century was the century of preservation. The roots of the appreciation of old buildings lie in eighteenth-century antiquarianism and in the emerging tourism during the Napoleonic Wars when, cut off from the continent, the English embarked on exploring their own country, and churches began to appear in guidebooks as objects of aesthetic, antiquarian and anecdotal interest. The rise of the preservation movement at the close of the Victorian period also affected the country church. The process began in 1877 with the foundation of the Society for the Protection of Ancient Buildings – directly precipitated by the ruthless 'restoration' of medieval churches

– and the passing of the Ancient Monuments Protection Act in 1882. In the next century there emerged the Georgian Society and then the Victorian Society. In recent times, the Historic Buildings Council, its successor, English Heritage and the Council for the Care of Churches are part of a long list of institutions and societies that try to stop the clock and whose permission must now be sought for any change in the physical appearance of the building. Until the twentieth century the country church could be altered and adapted in response to the religious changes that affected the Church of England. Now the church is all too often frozen in time. Preservation is admirable and essential in many areas but I wonder whether it really aids the survival of the country church. In recent years the word has begun to take on negative connotations and we should look for a replacement that indicates a desire to move on. Perhaps we need bodies whose names feature the word 'adaptation' rather than 'conservation' or 'preservation'.

Much has been achieved in recent years. Through the Historic Buildings Council and its successor, English Heritage, some £200 million have been allocated since 1977 to maintain and restore historic churches. But as it stands, the English Heritage money makes up only 6 per cent, and the Heritage Lottery Fund only 8 per cent of the total repair bill. The remaining about 85 per cent comes from the congregations and from members of the local community who love the buildings and wish them to survive. Thus many churches benefit from the fact that villages have become the province of the affluent middle classes who can afford to dig into their pockets: the reinvented village could well be the salvation of the English country church.

Churches don't have any of the problems that originally surrounded the country house: they are truly democratic buildings, the meeting place of ordinary people through the ages. For centuries the parish church was the only building large enough for the local community to gather not only for worship but for business and play. In the Middle Ages it was often the location of a school in a room over the porch. Mystery plays were performed here and the church also provided the setting for feasts until church ales were suppressed by the Puritans. But the Anglican Church followed the Puritan path and, by the late Victorian period, any activities not related to the church service were relocated to the newly built village hall. This concept of the church as sacred space has contributed to today's problems by divorcing religion from ordinary life: many battles over what is to happen to country churches stem from this fixed attitude that they should never be an arena for other activities. If the multiple use had been sustained there would have been no need for church halls. I believe that many problems could be solved today by giving the church building back to the local community, albeit with safeguards for worship. Through such adaptation the parish church could once again become a building for the community that is used for every kind of activity.

Change has been the lifeblood of the country church through the ages. If you walked into any of them over the centuries, you would have found them altered: either wholly or partially rebuilt, the interiors rearranged, some things kept, others discarded. If churches need to be given back to the communities that surround them, then the building cannot be regarded as untouchable and unalterable. Adaptation will be more important than preservation.

Not every building has a natural right to live on. The real challenge lies in giving the country church a *reason* to survive – and it is likely to be different from the reason why the church was originally built, now that the small, isolated rural community that once justified its existence has disappeared. We can no longer assume that all of these buildings will survive to the end of this century. Often the disappearance of a church is seen as yet another nail in the coffin of the Established Church – but it shouldn't be. Patterns of Christian worship have changed. The Christian faith moves on.

* * *

I end as I began with Philip Larkin's poem 'Church Going', written in 1954 when the problems were considerably less than they are now. It remains an extraordinary meditation on the loss of belief by someone who pushes open that church door.

> Yet stop I did: in fact, I often do,
> And always end much at a loss like this,
> Wondering what to look for; wondering, too,
> When churches fall completely out of use
> What we shall turn them into . . .
>
>   . . . I wonder who
> Will be the last, the very last, to seek
> This place for what it was; one of the crew
> That tap and jot and know what rood-lofts were?
> Some ruin-bibber, randy for antique,
> Or Christmas-addict, counting on a whiff
> Of gown-and-bands and organ-pipes and myrrh?
> Or will he be my representative,
>
> Bored, uninformed, knowing the ghostly silt
> Dispersed, yet tending to this cross of ground
> Through suburb scrub because it held unspoilt
> So long and equably what since is found
> Only in separation – marriage, and birth,
> And death, and thoughts of these – for which was built
> This special shell? For, though I've no idea
> What this accoutred frowsty barn is worth,
> It pleases me to stand in silence here . . .

Bibliography

I HAVE MARKED WITH AN asterisk those titles that I found of particular use, especially the pioneering studies of various localities.

*Addleshaw, G. W. O., and Frederick Etchells, *The Architectural Setting of Anglican Worship*, Faber & Faber, 1948

Alexander, Jonathan, and Paul Binski (eds), *Age of Chivalry: Art in England 1200–1400*, Royal Academy Exhibition Catalogue, 1987

*Anson, Peter F., *Fashions in Church Furnishings 1840–1940*, Studio Vista, 1965

Arnoult, Sharon L., '"Spiritual and Sacred Publique Actions": *The Book of Common Prayer* and the Understanding of Worship in the Elizabethan and Jacobean Church of England', in E. J. Carlson (ed.), *Religion and the English People 1500–1640: New Voices, New Perspectives*, Sixteenth-Century Essays & Studies, 45, 1998, pp. 25–47

Aston, Margaret, 'Iconoclasm: Official and Clandestine', in *idem, Faith and Fire: Popular and Unpopular Religion 1350–1600*, Hambledon Press, 1993, pp. 261–89

Atherton, Ian, 'Viscount Scudamore's "Laudianism": The Religious Position of the First Viscount Scudamore', *Historical Journal*, 34:3, 1991, pp. 567–96

Bainbridge, Virginia R., *Gilds in the Medieval Countryside: Social and Religious Change in Cambridgeshire, c. 1350–1558*, Boydell Press, 1996

Bax, B. Anthony, *The English Parsonage*, John Murray, 1964

*Beaver, Daniel C., *Parish Communities and Religious Conflict in the Vale of Gloucester 1590–1690*, Harvard University Press, 1998

*Betjeman, John (ed.), *The Collins Guide to English Parish Churches*, Collins, 1958

*—, *Trains and Buttered Toast*, ed. Stephen Games, John Murray, 2006

Blair, John (ed.), *Minsters and Parish Churches: The Local Church in Transition 950–1200*, Oxford University Committee for Archaeology, monograph no. 17, 1988

*—, and Richard Sharpe (eds), *Pastoral Care before the Parish*, Leicester University Press, 1992

The Book of Common Prayer, intro. Diarmaid MacCulloch, Everyman, 1999

Bossy, John, 'The Mass as a Social Institution 1200–1700', *Past & Present*, 100, 1983, pp. 29–61

*—, 'The Social History of Confession in the Age of the Reformation', *Transactions of the Royal Historical Society*, 5th series, 1975, pp. 21–38

Brigden, Susan, *London and the Reformation*, Clarendon Press, 1989

Brinkworth, E. R. C., 'The Laudian Church in Buckinghamshire', *University of Birmingham Historical Journal*, 5:2, 1955–6, pp. 31–59

Brooke, Christopher, 'Religious Sentiment and Church Design in the Middle Ages', in *idem*, *Medieval Church and Society*, Sidgwick & Jackson, 1971

*Brooks, Chris, and Andrew Saint (eds), *The Victorian Church: Architecture and Society*, Manchester University Press, 1995

*Brown, Andrew D., *Popular Piety in Late Medieval England: The Diocese of Salisbury 1250–1550*, Clarendon Press, 1995

Carlson, Eric Josef, '"Practical Divinity": Richard Greenham's Ministry in Elizabethan England', in *idem* (ed.), *Religion and the English People, 1500–1640: New Voices, New Perspectives*, Sixteenth-Century Essays & Studies, 45, 1998, pp. 147–93

*Collin, Irene, *Jane Austen and the Clergy*, Hambledon Press, 1993

Collinson, Patrick, *The Birth Pangs of Protestant England: Religious and Cultural Change in the Sixteenth and Seventeenth Centuries*, Macmillan, 1988

—, 'The Elizabethan Church and the New Religion', in Christopher Haigh (ed.), *The Reign of Elizabeth*, Macmillan, 1984, pp. 159–94

—, *The Religion of Protestants: The Church in English Society 1559–1625*, Clarendon Press, 1982

*Cressy, David, *Birth, Marriage, and Death: Ritual, Religion, and the Life-cycle in Tudor and Stuart Britain*, Oxford University Press, 1997

*—, *Bonfires and Bells: National Memory and the Protestant Calendar in Elizabethan and Stuart England*, Sutton, 1989

—, *Travesties and Transgressions in Tudor and Stuart England*, Oxford University Press, 2000

Cuming, G. J., *A History of Anglican Liturgy*, Macmillan, 1969

Cupitt, Don, *Radicals and the Future of the Church*, SCM Press, 1989

Davies, Horton, *Worship and Theology in England, 1690–1850*, Princeton University Press, 1961

—, *Worship and Theology in England, 1850–1900*, Princeton University Press, 1962

—, *Worship and Theology in England from Cranmer to Hooker 1534–1603*, Princeton University Press, 1970

—, *Worship and Theology in England from Andrewes to Baxter and Fox 1603–90*, Princeton University Press, 1975

*Davies, J. G., *The Secular Use of Church Buildings*, SCM Press, 1968

*Davies, Julian, *The Caroline Captivity of the Church: Charles I and the Remoulding of Anglicanism 1625–41*, Clarendon Press, 1992

Dillow, Kevin B., 'The Social and Ecclesiastical Significance of Church Seating Arrangements and Pew Disputes 1500–1740', D.Phil thesis, Merton College, Oxford, 1990

Doll, Peter, *After the Primitive Christians: The Eighteenth-Century Anglican Eucharist in its Architectural Setting*, Grove Books, 1997

*Duffy, Eamon, *The Stripping of the Altars: Traditional Religion in England, c. 1400–c. 1580*, Yale University Press, 1992

*—, *The Voices of Morebath: Reformation and Rebellion in an English Village*, Yale University Press, 2003

Ellman, Edward Boys, *Recollections of a Sussex Parson*, Skeffington & Son, 1912

English Romanesque Art 1066–1200, Hayward Gallery Exhibition Catalogue, 1984

Fielding, John, 'Arminianism in the Localities: Peterborough Diocese 1603–1642', in Kenneth Fincham (ed.), *The Early Stuart Church*, Macmillan, 1993, pp. 93–113

Foster, Richard, *Discovering English Churches*, BBC Books, 1981

*French, Katherine L., *The People of the Parish: Community Life in a Late Medieval English Diocese*, University of Pennsylvania Press, 2000

*Gibbs, Gary G., and Beat A. Kumin (eds), *The Parish in English Life 1400–1600*, Manchester University Press, 1997

Godfrey, John, *The Church in Anglo-Saxon England*, Cambridge University Press, 1962

Gothic: Art for England 1400–1547, ed. Richard Marks and Paul Williamson, Victoria and Albert Museum Exhibition Catalogue, 2003

Gough, Richard, *The History of Myddle*, ed. David Hey, Folio Society, 1958

Graves, C. P., 'Social Space in the English Medieval Church', *Economy and Society*, 18, 1989, pp. 297–322

Green, Ian, '"For Children in Yeeres and Children in Understanding": The Emergence of the English Catechism under Elizabeth and the Early Stuarts', *Journal of Ecclesiastical History*, 37:3, 1986, pp. 397–425

*Gregory, Jeremy, *Restoration, Reformation and Reform, 1660–1828: Archbishops of Canterbury and Their Diocese*, Clarendon Press, 2000

—, and Jeffrey S. Chamberlain (eds), *The National Church in Local Perspective: The Church of England and the Regions, 1660–1800*, Boydell Press, 2003

Haigh, Christopher, 'The Church of England, the Catholics and the People', in Christopher Haigh (ed.), *The Reign of Elizabeth I*, Macmillan, 1984, pp. 195–219

*— (ed.), *The English Reformation Revised*, Cambridge University Press, 1987

—, *English Reformations: Religion, Politics and Society under the Tudors*, Clarendon Press, 1993

*Hammond, Peter C., *The Parson and the Victorian Parish*, Hodder & Stoughton, 1977

Hardy, W. J., 'Remarks on the History of Seat-reservation in Churches', *Archaeologia*, 2nd series, 3, 1892, pp. 95–106

Heal, Felicity, *Reformation in Britain and Ireland*, Oxford University Press, 2003

Hunt, Arnold, 'The Lord's Supper in Early Modern England', *Past & Present*, 161, 1998, pp. 39–83

Ingram, Martin, 'From Reformation to Toleration: Popular Religious Cultures in England, 1540–1690', in Tim Harris (ed.), *Popular Culture in England, c. 1500–1850*, Macmillan, 1995, pp. 95–123

*Jenkins, Simon, *England's Thousand Best Churches*, Penguin, 1999

Knight, Frances, 'The Influence of the Oxford Movement in the Parishes, c. 1833–1860', in Paul Vass (ed.), *From Oxford to the People*, Gracewing, 1996, pp. 127–40

*Kumin, Beat A., *The Shaping of a Community: The Rise and Reformation of the English Parish, c. 1400–1560*, Scolar Press, 1996

Lake, Peter, 'The Laudian Style: Order, Uniformity and the Pursuit of the Beauty of Holiness in the 1630s', in Kenneth Fincham (ed.), *The Early Stuart Church*, Macmillan, 1993, pp. 161–85

*Litzenberger, Caroline, *The English Reformation and the Laity: Gloucestershire, 1540–1580*, Cambridge University Press, 1997

Maltby, Judith, '"By this Book": Parishioners, the Prayer Book and the Established Church', in Kenneth Fincham (ed.) *The Early Stuart Church*, Macmillan, 1993, pp. 115–37

*—, *Prayer Book and People in Elizabethan and Early Stuart England*, Cambridge University Press, 1998

Marchant, R. A., 'The Restoration of Nottinghamshire Churches, 1635–40', *Thoroton Society Transactions*, 1961, pp. 57–93

Marsh, Christopher, '"Common Prayer" in England 1560–1640: The View from the Pew', *Past & Present*, 171, 2001, pp. 66–94

*—, *Popular Religion in Sixteenth-Century England*, St Martin's Press, 1998

Mason, Emma, 'The Role of the English Parishioner, 1000–1500', *Journal of Ecclesiastical History*, 27, 1976, pp. 17–29

Mather, F. C., 'Georgian Churchmanship Reconsidered: Some Variations in Anglican Public Worship 1714–1830', *Journal of Ecclesiastical History*, 36:2, 1995, pp. 255–83

Maxwell, William D., *An Outline of Christian Worship*, Oxford University Press, 1936

Morrill, John, 'The Church in England 1642–1649', in *idem*, *The Nature of the English Revolution*, Longman, 1993

Morris, Jeremy, 'The Regional Growth of Tractarianism: Some Reflections', in Paul Vass (ed.), *From Oxford to the People*, Gracewing, 1996, pp. 141–59

Morris, R. K., 'The Church in the Countryside: Two Lines of Inquiry', in D. Hooke (ed.), *Medieval Villages*, Oxford University Committee for Archaeology, monograph no. 5, 1985

Nichols, Ann Eljenholm, *Seeable Signs: The Iconography of the Seven Sacraments 1350–1544*, Boydell Press, 1994

*Obelkevich, James, *Religion and Rural Society: South Lindsey 1825–1875*, Cambridge University Press, 1976

Orme, Nicholas, *Medieval Children*, Yale University Press, 2001

Parker, Sir William, *The History of Long Melford*, Wyman & Sons, 1873

Peters, Christine, *Patterns of Piety: Women, Gender and Religion in Late Medieval and Reformation England*, Cambridge University Press, 2003

Phillips, C. H., *The Singing Church: An Outline of the Music Sung by Choir and People*, revised edition, ed. Arthur Hutchings, Faber & Faber, 1968

Phillips, John, *The Reformation of Images: Destruction of Art in England 1535–1660*, University of California Press, 1973

Powys, A. R., *The English Parish Church*, Longmans, Green & Co., 1930

*Rosman, Doreen, *The Evolution of the English Churches 1500–2000*, Cambridge University Press, 2003

Rosser, Gervase, 'Communities of Parish and Guild in the Late Middle Ages', in S. J. Wright (ed.), *Parish, Church and People: Local Studies in Lay Religion 1350–1750*, Hutchinson, 1988

Simmons, T. F. (ed.), *The Lay Folks Mass Book*, Early English Text Society, 71, 1879

*Spaeth, Donald A., *The Church in an Age of Danger: Parsons and Parishioners, 1660–1740*, Cambridge University Press, 2000

—, 'Common Prayer? Popular Observance of the Anglican Liturgy in Restoration Wiltshire', in S. J. Wright (ed.), *Parish, Church and People: Local Studies in Lay Religion 1350–1750*, Hutchinson, 1988

*Spinks, Bryan, *Sacraments, Ceremonies and the Stuart Divines: Sacramental Theology and Liturgy in England and Scotland 1603–1662*, Ashgate, 2002

Spufford, Margaret, *Contrasting Communities: English Villagers in the Sixteenth and Seventeenth Centuries*, Sutton, 2000

*Temperley, Nicholas, *The Music of the English Parish Church*, Cambridge University Press, 1979

Thomson, John A. F., *The Early Tudor Church and Society 1485–1529*, Longman, 1993

Tindal Hart, A., *The Country Clergy in Elizabethan and Stuart Times*, Phoenix House, 1958

—, *The Country Priest in English History*, Phoenix House, 1959

—, *The Eighteenth-Century Country Parson, c. 1689 to 1830*, Wilding & Son, 1955

—, *The Man in the Pew 1558–1660*, John Baker, 1966

—, and Edward Carpenter, *The Nineteenth-Century Country Parson, c. 1832–1900*, Wilding & Son, 1954

*Tyacke, Nicholas, *Anti-Calvinists: The Rise of English Arminianism c. 1590–1640*, Clarendon Press, 1987

*Virgin, Peter, *The Church in an Age of Negligence*, James Clarke & Co., 1989

*Walsham, Alexandra, *Church Papists: Catholicism, Conformity and Confessional Polemic in Modern England*, Royal Historical Society, Boydell Press, 1993

*Warmington, A. R., *Civil War, Interregnum and Restoration in Gloucestershire 1640–1672*, Boydell Press, 1997

White, C. H. Evelyn, 'The Journal of William Dowsing . . .', *Proceedings of the Suffolk Institute of Archaeology and Natural History*, 6, 1888, pp. 236–90

Woodforde, James, *The Diary of a Country Parson 1758–1802*, ed. John Beresford, Oxford University Press, 1972

Wright, S. J., 'Confirmation, Catechism and Communion: The Role of the Young in the Post-Reformation Church', in S. J. Wright (ed.), *Parish, Church and People: Local Studies in Lay Religion 1350–1750*, Hutchinson, 1988

Wrightson, Keith, 'The Politics of the Parish in Early Modern England', in Paul Griffiths, Adam Fox and Steve Hindle (eds), *The Experience of Authority in Early Modern England*, Basingstoke, 1996

*Yates, Nigel, *Buildings, Faith, and Worship: The Liturgical Arrangement of Anglican Churches*, Clarendon Press, 1991

List of Illustrations

Colour plate section

1   Detail from a Doom painting, fifteenth century, St Peter, Wenhaston, Suffolk. © Derek Anson/E&E Image Library.

2   St Michael, painted screen, fifteenth century, St Helen, Ranworth, Norfolk. © Angelo Hornak Photograph Library.

3   Baptism, stained glass, fifteenth century, detail from the Seven Sacraments window, St Michael, Doddiscombsleigh, Devon. © Helen McClement/E&E Image Library.

4   Sir Henry Unton's funeral, 1596, detail from *Sir Henry Unton*, painting by an unknown artist. © National Portrait Gallery, London.

5   *Coming from Evening Church*, 1830, painting by Samuel Palmer. © Tate London 2007.

6   *The Reverend and Mrs Thomas Gisborne, of Yoxhall Lodge, Leicestershire*, 1786, painting by Joseph Wright of Derby. © Yale Center for British Art, Paul Mellon Collection, USA/Bridgeman Art Library.

7   *A Sleepy Congregation*, watercolour by Thomas Rowlandson (1756–1827). © Private Collection/Bridgeman Art Library.

8   *Yorkshire Dales*, 1961, poster by Ronald Lampitt produced for British Railways. © Science & Society Picture Library/NRM Pictorial Collection.

Illustrations in the text

iii   *On the Way to Church, the South Downs*, painting by Robert Gallon (*fl.* 1868–1905). © Private Collection/Fine Art Photographic Library.

5   St Nicholas, Barfreston, Kent. Edwin Smith/RIBA Library, Photographs Collection.

11   Central motif of mosaic pavement, fourth century, from the villa at Hinton St Mary, Dorset. © Dorset Country Museum/ Bridgeman Art Library.

14   Earth Mother corbel, St Mary and St David, Kilpeck, Herefordshire. © Steve Sant/Alamy.

15   Chancel, St Mary and St David, Kilpeck, Herefordshire. Edwin Smith/RIBA Library, Photographs Collection.

16   Celtic cross, Holy Island, Lindisfarne. © Steve Allen Travel Photography/Alamy.

19   St Laurence, Bradford-on-Avon, Wiltshire. Edwin Smith/ RIBA Library, Photographs Collection.

22   St Peter, Barton upon Humber, Humberside. © Florian Monheim/Alamy.

25   Chalice, *c.* 1200. © The Trustees of the British Museum. Paten, *c.* 1280, St Matthew's Wyke, Winchester, Hampshire.

27   Font, twelfth century, St Michael, Castle Frome, Herefordshire. © Angelo Hornak Photograph Library.

28   Tympanum, *c.* 1140, St Mary, Fownhope, Herefordshire. © Angelo Hornak Photograph Library.

29   Priest baptising an infant, mid-fourteenth-century manuscript. Royal 6.E.VI. © The British Library Board. All rights reserved.

32   Holy Trinity, Long Melford, Suffolk. © Les Polders/Alamy.

33   Rood-screen, fifteenth century, St Helen, Ranworth, Norfolk. Edwin Smith/RIBA Library, Photographs Collection.

34   Figure of crucified Christ from a rood-screen, early sixteenth century, St Anthony, Cartmel Fell, Cumbria (on loan to the Kendal Museum).

35   English chasuble, mid-fifteenth century © V&A Images/ Victoria and Albert Museum, London.

37   Mass from an English primer, fifteenth century. Classmark Sel.5.35. Reproduced by permission of the Syndics of Cambridge University Library.

41   Doom painting, fifteenth century, St Peter and St Paul, Chaldon, Surrey. Edwin Smith/RIBA Library, Photographs Collection.

42   Nave roof, fifteenth century, St Wendreda, March, Cambridgeshire. Edwin Smith/RIBA Library, Photographs Collection.

43   Alabaster figure of Virgin and Child, fifteenth century. © The Trustees of the British Museum.

45   Wall paintings, mid-fourteenth century, St Mary, Chalgrove, Oxfordshire. Reproduced by permission of English Heritage/ NMR.

47   Early Tudor porch, St Mary, Radwinter, Essex. © Paul Barker.

49   John Waymont and his wife at the feet of St Jerome and St Ambrose entreat the passer-by to pray for their souls, painted screen, St Thomas, Foxley, Norfolk. © Angelo Hornak Photograph Library.

51   Wooden pax, *c.* 1500, St Andrew, Sandon, Essex.

54   Easter sepulchre, fifteenth century, St Patrick, Patrington, Humberside. © A. F. Kersting.

56   Priest celebrates Mass, mid-fourteenth-century manuscript. Roy 6.E.VI. © The British Library Board. All rights reserved.

57   Priest gives communion, mid-fourteenth-century manuscript. Roy 6.E.VI. © The British Library Board. All rights reserved.

59   Thomas Peyton and wives, fifteenth-century brass rubbing, Isleham, Cambridgeshire.

61   Woodcut from John Foxe, *Actes and Monuments*, 1563.

64   St Mary, Fairford, Gloucestershire. © Michael Jenner/Alamy.

68   Parish chest, fifteenth century. © A. F. Kersting.

73   Defaced images, St Peter, Ringland, Norfolk. Reproduced by permission of English Heritage/NMR.

74   The destruction of traditional religion, from John Foxe, *Actes and Monuments*, 1563.

76   The new religion, from John Foxe, *Actes and Monuments*, 1563.

77   Head of Christ, wood fragment of a crucifix, 1101–1125. © The Trustees of the British Museum.

79   Make-shift painted Rood, St Catherine, Ludham, Norfolk. Edwin Smith/RIBA Library, Photographs Collection.

81   Arms of Elizabeth I, St Catherine, Ludham, Norfolk. Edwin Smith/RIBA Library, Photographs Collection.

83   Edward VI presents the Bible to his people, from John Foxe, *Actes and Monuments*, 1563.

85   *The holie Bible*, 1568. c.35.l.14. © The British Library Board. All rights reserved.

88   St Issui, Partrishow, Herefordshire. © John Heseltine/Corbis.

90   Receiving Holy Communion, from Richard Day, *A Booke of Christian Prayers*, 1578.

92   *Love of God*, from Richard Day, *A Booke of Christian Prayers*, 1578.

94   The new religion of the Word, from John Foxe, *Actes and Monuments*, 1563.

95   The Protestant view of the old religion, from John Foxe, *Actes and Monuments*, 1563.

100   *The Book of Common Prayer*, 1549. © Private Collection/ Bridgeman Art Library

102   Chancel, Hailes Church, Gloucestershire. Reproduced by kind permission of the Cathedral and Church Buildings Division of the Archbishop's Council.

105   Baptism, from Richard Day, *A Booke of Christian Prayers*, 1578.

107   Catechising, from Richard Day, *A Booke of Christian Prayers*, 1578.

113   Tombs of the earls of Rutland, St Mary the Virgin, Bottesford, Leicestershire. © Martin Charles.

115   St Andrew, Westhall, Suffolk. Edwin Smith/RIBA Library, Photographs Collection.

117   Burning of Protestant martyrs, from John Foxe, *Actes and Monuments*, 1563.

119   Communion for the sick, from Richard Day, *A Booke of Christian Prayers*, 1578.

121   Anglican Gothic window, Low Ham, Somerset. © A. F. Kersting.

124   St Mary, Abbey Dore, Herefordshire. © Isobel Sindon/E&E Image Library.

128   Authorised version of the Bible, 1611. C.35.l.11. © The British Library Board. All rights reserved.

130   Holy Communion, from *The Christian's Jewel*, 1624.

133   St Michael, Rycote, Oxfordshire. © A. F. Kersting.

135   Anglican Gothic ceiling, 1637, St Mary, East Brent, Somerset. © A. F. Kersting.

140   Baptism, from *The Christian Jewel*, 1624.

141   Gilt chalice with paten cover, 1640, All Saints, Mugginton, Derby.

143   Burning of popish pictures, 1643. Private Collection.

146   St Barnabas, Brampton Bryan, Herefordshire. Reproduced by permission of English Heritage/NMR.

147   Holy Trinity, Staunton Harold, Leicestershire. © John Bethell/National Trust Photo Library.

150   Mutilated sculpture, St Cuthbert, Wells, Somerset. Conway Library, Courtauld Institute of Arts, London/Canon M. H. Ridgway.

152   Destruction of the 'beauty of holiness', seventeenth century. Private Collection.

154   Anti-Puritan tract, 1641. Private Collection.

161   Corpse in a reusable coffin, engraving, *c.* 1657. Private Collection.

163   Scene from the life of Christ, mutilated sandstone relief, *c.* 1155. Reproduced by kind permission of the Dean and Chapter, Durham Cathedral.

165   *Choristers*, *c.* 1812, drawing by John Nixon. © Torre Abbey, Torquay, Devon/Bridgeman Art Library.

168   St John the Baptist, Mildenhall, Wiltshire. © Paul Barker/ Country Life Picture Library.

172   Receiving Holy Communion, from Lancelot Addison, *An Introduction to the Sacrament*, 1693.

176–7   Seating in the church at Myddle, Shropshire, from Richard Gough, *Observations concerning the Seates in Myddle and the families to which they belong*, 1701. Facsimile reproduced from The Folio Society edition, edited by David Hey, 1983.

178   Villagers present their tithe, Derby porcelain group, *c.* 1775. © Lincolnshire County Council, Usher Gallery, Lincoln/ Bridgeman Art Library.

181   Journeyman parson and master parson, *c.* 1782, caricatures by Robert Dighton. © The Trustees of the British Museum.

184   Holy Communion, from Charles Wheatly, *A Rational Illustration of the Book of Common Prayer*, 1714 edition.

187   Matins in a country church, 1790, print by J. Wright. © The Trustees of the British Museum.

188   St John the Baptist, King's Norton, Leicestershire. Reproduced by permission of English Heritage/NMR.

193   *Village Choir, c.* 1770, print by Samuel H. Grimm. © The Trustees of the British Museum.

195   Master parson and his journeyman, 1812, caricature by Robert Dighton. © The Trustees of the British Museum.

197   The 'correct' altar, 1847, Cambridge Camden Society.

201   Holy Innocents, Higham, Gloucestershire. © R. J. L. Smith, Much Wenlock, Shropshire.

205   Parish vestry meeting, *c.* 1784, watercolour by Thomas Rowlandson. © V&A Images/Victoria and Albert Museum. London.

209   Drawings of Bicknor Church, Kent. EK/U449/P6. East Kent Archives Centre.

211   Stained glass, *c.* 1890, by Sir Edward Burne-Jones, St Margaret, Rottingdean, East Sussex. Martyn O'Kelly/Bridgeman Art Library.

212–13 Church interior before and after reordering, cartoons from *The Reformation and the Deformation*, 1868, by Mowbray of Oxford.

215   *A Procession before the Eucharist,* 1906, by Simon Harman Vedder, reproduced in Percy Dearmer, *The Parson's Handbook*, 1932.

219   *The Village Choir*, painting by John Watkins Chapman (*fl.* 1853–1903). © Christie's Images Ltd.

221   *Christening Sunday, South Harting, Sussex*, 1887, painting by

James Charles. © Manchester Art Gallery/Bridgeman Art Library.

223 Congregation singing, engraving, 1881. © Mary Evans Picture Library.

225 *St Nicholas, Alcester*, 1985, watercolour by John Piper. © Private Collection/Crane Kalman/Bridgeman Art Library. Reproduced by kind permission of the Piper Estate.

236 *May Day*, painting by Joseph Francis Nollekens (1702–48). © Private Collection/Bridgeman Art Library.

Index

Abbey Dore, Herefordshire 123–5, *124*, 141

Acts of Parliament
  Act in Restraint of Appeals (1529) 66
  Act of Convocation (1536) 80
  Act of Supremacy (1534) 80
  Act of Uniformity/Elizabethan Settlement (1559) 89, 91, 95, 96, 97–8, 103, 119, 125, 136, 213; (1662) 168, 171
  Act of Uniformity Amendment Act (1872) 216
  Ancient Monuments Protection Act (1882) 233
  Burial Act (1880) 220
  Catholic Emancipation Act (1829) 202
  Conventicle Act (1664) 168–9
  Education Act (1944) 231
  Five Mile Act (1665) 169
  Local Government Act (1894) 205
  Marriage Act (1753) 190
  Marriage and Registration Act (1653) 160
  Parochial Libraries Act (1709) 173
  Pluralities Act (1838) 206
  Test Act (1673) 169
  Test and Corporation Act (1828) 202
  Tithe Acts (1696) 178–9
  Toleration Act (1689) 170, 171, 175

Addison, Joseph 173
advowsons 174, 205
Adwick le Street, South Yorkshire 70
agrarian revolution 204
Alcock, John, bishop of Ely 40
ales, church 58, 75, 80, 99, 126, 127, 170
All Saints' Day 52, 67, 82
All Souls' Day 52
Allerton, Northumberland 103
Alpha Course, the 231
altarage 58
altarpieces 59, 185

altars 26, 39, 78, 87, 97, 101, 123–4, 174, 210, 213, *213*, 230
  abolition of 72, 73, 76, 83, 148
  candles and candlesticks 28, 131, 185, 216
  rails 124, 134, 138, 148, 174, 185
  see also Holy Tables
ambo 186
Ambrose, St 44, 63
Ancient Monuments Protection Act (1882) 233
Andrewes, Lancelot, bishop of Winchester 129, 130, 131, 132, 137
  private chapel 133–4, *135*
angels, images of 23, 41, *42*, 44, 65, *133*
Anglican Church *see* Church of England
Anglo-Catholics 204, 217
Anglo-Saxon churches *19*, 19–20, *22*
Annunciation, the 118
Apollonia, St 41
Aquinas, St Thomas 39
arches, chancel 13, *15*, 21, 22, 23
arms *see* coats of arms
Ascension Day/Ascensiontide 67, 222
Ash Wednesday 18, 70, 117
asperges 44
Assumption of the Virgin 52
attendance, church 10, 23, 93, 95–6, 98, 107, 111, 171–2, 187, 208, 230
Augustine, St 13, 16, 17, 21, 23, 24, 44, 63, 129
aumbries 27
Austen, Jane: family connections 179–80

Bancroft, Richard, Archbishop of Canterbury 127, 128
bands, village 192
baptism 23, 28, 44–6, 55, 67, 73, 91, *105*, 108, 109, 118, 126, 132, *140*, 148, 157, 158–9
Baptists 155, 157, 169, 170, 202

Barbara, St 44
Barton upon Humber, Humberside: St Peter 22, *22*
basilicas, Christian 21, 22
Beccles Church, Suffolk 151
Becket, St Thomas 25
Beckington Church, Somerset 139–40
bede-rolls 48, 101
bells 18, *52*, 55, 67, 75, 82, 118, 126, 138, 216
Bemerton, Wiltshire: rectory 207
bequests 75, 98–9
Berwick Church, Sussex 222
Betjeman, John 8–9
Bible, the 14, 36–7, 67, 69, 76, 80, 101–2, 114, 116–17, 230, 231
    Authorised Version (1611) 128, *128*, 131, 195, 228
    Biblia Pauperum 63
    Coverdale 67
Bicknor Church, Kent *209*
Bingham, Joseph: *Origines Ecclesiasticae: or, The Antiquities of the Christian Church* 186
Blomfield, A. W. 208
Bodley, G. F. 208, *209*
Boleyn, Anne 66, 77
Book of Common Prayer/Prayer Books (1549) 71, 82, 83, 89, 90, *100*, 101; (1552) 71, 73, 89–90, 99, 101; (1559) 71, 96, 98, 99, 101, 102, 103, 106, 107, 114; (1604) 71, 118, 126–7, 129, 130, 140–41, 148, 153, 155–6, 163; (1662) 71, 168, 170, 171, 228, 229
Books of Hours 36
Boothby Pagnell Church, Lincolnshire 155–6
Bottesford, Leicestershire: St Mary the Virgin *113*
Bound, Nicholas: *The Doctrine of the Sabbath* 126
Bradford-on-Avon, Wiltshire: St Laurence *19*, 23
Brampton Bryan, Herefordshire: St Barnabas 145–6, *146*
brasses 59, 63
Brent, Sir Nathaniel 140
Bressingham, Norfolk: guilds 38
Brictric (priest) 25–6

'Broad Church' 216
Burial Act (1880) 220, 222
burials/funerals 20, 38, 40–1, 55, 56, 58–9, 68, 74, 82, 148, 157, 160–2, *161*, 191, 207, 220, 222
Burne-Jones, Sir Edward: stained glass window *211*
Burnet, Gilbert, bishop of Salisbury: *Discourse of the Pastoral Care* 180, 182
Burton Latimer, Northamptonshire 134
Butterfield, William 200, 208, 218–19
Byrd, William 217

Caldecote, Cambridgeshire 155
Calvinism 90, 96, 126
Cambridge Camden (*later* Ecclesiological) Society 200, 210, 214–15
Cambridgeshire *42*, 133, 134, 138, 155, 156, 212
Candlemas 44, 52, 67, 70, 117
candles and candlesticks 28, 34, 50, 58, 63, 98, 131, 151, 185, 199, 211, 213, 228
    votive 65, 66, 68, 69, 216
    see also Candlemas
Canons: (1571) 103; (1603) 114; (1604) 94, 97, 127–8, 130, 135, 136, 158
Canterbury, Kent 189
    Archbishops *see* Bancroft, Richard; Cranmer, Thomas; Laud, William; Parker, Matthew; Secker, Thomas; Wake, William
    Cathedral 25, 67
Cantilupe, St Thomas 41
Cartwright, Thomas 93–4
Castle Frome, Herefordshire: St Michael 27
catechism 67, *107*, 107–8, 137, 190–91, 220
Catholic Church
    under Elizabeth I 89–94, 95–6, 114, 116–19, 169
    under Mary I 77–8
    and Reformation 66, 81, *see* Reformation
    in seventeenth and eighteenth centuries 169–70, 173, 190, 191, 194
    in nineteenth century 202–3
Catholic Emancipation Act (1829) 202
Caxton, William: *Doctrinal of Sapience* 50

Celtic Church 16, 17, 18
Celtic crosses 16, *16*, 22
Central Advisory Council of Training for
    the Ministry 208
Chaldon, Surrey: St Peter and St Paul *41*
Chalgrove, Oxfordshire: St Mary 44, *45*
chalices *25*, 27, 33, 50, 76, 114, 131, 133,
    216, 230
chancels 22, 26, 27, *102*, 108, 137, 138–9,
    210, 212, 214
    arched 13, *15*, 21, 22, 23
    decorated with Gospel cycle 44, *45*
    and rood-screens 32, *33*
chantries and chantry chapels 39–40, 59,
    63, 69–70, 75, 82, 105
Charles I 125, 129, 138, 147, 148, 155,
    171
Charles II 169, 171
Chaucer, Geoffrey: *Canterbury Tales* 47, 65
Chester, Cheshire: rood-lofts 92–3
Chichester, Sussex 94
    training college 208
chi-rho monogram 16
choirs/choristers 35, 78, 192–4, *193*, 214,
    216, *219*, 228
chrism 46
chrisom cloth 46, 47, 160
Christening Sunday *221*
christenings *see* baptisms
Christian, Ewan 208
Christians, early 14, 16, 21, 129, 183,
    185, 186
Christmas 52, 71, 103, 118, 151, 155,
    189, 190
Christopher, St 41
church: etymology 21
church ales *see* ales, church
church building and repairs 20, 22, 70,
    111–12, 130, 131–2, 208–9, 212–13,
    231–3
Church Leighton, Leicestershire 180
Church of England/Anglican Church 75,
    90, 94–5, 98, 114, 116–19, 129,
    229–31
    Six Articles (1539) 69
    Ten Articles (1536) 67
    in seventeenth century 131, 132–5,
        137–41, 146–9, 156–7, 168–70
    in nineteenth century 200, 202–3; *see
        also* Oxford Movement; Victorian era

see also Book of Common Prayer;
    Canons; communion; Puritans;
    Reformation
churchings 46–7, 55, 126, 127, 148, 157,
    160, 207
churchwardens 26, 58, 68, 75–6, 82, 98,
    110, 111, 114, 139–40, 174–5
    accounts 58, 78, 80
churchyards 26, 52, 55, 58, 70, 114, 175
Civil War, English 71, 75, 123, 145, 147,
    151, 156, 163, 171
Clapham Sect 202
clerestories 23
clergy (parsons, priests, vicars)
    celibacy 25, 36, 69, 112
    education 57, 172, 180, 208
    in eighteenth and nineteenth centuries
        179–80, *181*, 182–3, 218
    income 25–6, 57–8, 112, 175, 178–9,
        206, 207
    medieval 25–7, *56*, 56–7, *57*, 102
    non-resident 178, 206
Cloud of Unknowing (anon.) 38
coats of arms 59, 112
    royal *80*, 87, 108, 116, 171, 185
*Collins Guide to English Parish
    Churches, The* (ed. Betjeman) 9
Common Worship 229–30
communion/Holy Communion 17, 50, *57*,
    58
    bread and wine 50, 51–2, 70, 71, 73, 75,
        89, 90, 93, 104, 133, 138, 216
    in sixteenth and seventeenth centuries
        73, 89, *90*, 93, 101, *102*, 103–4, 107,
        108, 118, 127, 130, 155, 162–3, *172*
    in eighteenth century 169, 183, *184*,
        189–90
    in nineteenth century 218, *219*
    in twentieth century 229
    see also chalices
Compton Abdale, Gloucestershire 93
confession 50–51, 69, 191
    see also Confiteor
confirmation 46, 55, 74, 190, 220
Confiteor 18, 48
Congregationalists 169, 170, 202
Consistory Court of York 194
Constantine I, Emperor 14
Conventicle Act (1664) 168–9
conventicles 111

Convocations 98, 127
Cooper, Reverend Dr Edward 179
Cooper, Reverend Edward 179
corbels 13, *14*, 65
Cornwall 71, 206
Corpus Christi 34, *35*, 38, 52, 117, 136
Council for the Care of Churches 233
Coverdale, Miles: Bible 67
Cranmer, Thomas, Archbishop of
  Canterbury 69, 89, 99, 103, 106, 138
Creed, the 18, 28, 48, 67, 80, 87, 98, 107,
  116, 126, 127, 153
Cromwell, Oliver 145, 148, 149, 155, 163
Cromwell, Thomas 67, 69, 80
crosses/Crucifixes 33, *34*, 70, 151,
  158
  Celtic 16, *16*, 22
  see also Roods
Crundale Church, Kent 173
Cuddesdon, Oxfordshire: training college
  208
curates 68, 110, 178, *181*, 183

dalmatics *35*, 185
Dark Ages 16
Darwinism 217
Daynes, Reverend Thomas 127
Dearmer, Percy: *The Parson's Handbook*
  214, *215*
death and the dead 38, 39, 47–8, 70, 89,
  118
  see also burials/funerals
Decalogue *see* Ten Commandments
Declarations of Indulgence: (1672) 169;
  (1687) 169
Decorated style 210, 228
'de Coverley, Sir Roger' 173–4
Devon 71–2, 81–3, 97–9, 189
Directory of Public Worship 153, 156, 158,
  160, 162, 191
Dissenters 169, 170, 172, 173, 178, 191,
  202
Donne, John 156
Doom paintings 40, *41*
Dowsing, William 151–3
Duffy, Eamon: *The Stripping of the
  Altars* 2, 80, 82, 97–9
Duncombe family 180
Durham Cathedral 25, 67, 134

Earle, John: *Microcosmography* 95
Earls Colne, Essex 109–10
East Brent, Somerset: St Mary *135*
East Retford Church, Nottinghamshire
  138
Easter 17, 50, 52, 55, 71, 103, 114, 118,
  127, 162, 189, 208, 219
Easter Sepulchres 32–3, 53, *54*, 55, 65,
  70, 82, 83, 97, 117
Ecclesiastical Commission 93
ecclesiological movement 210, 212,
  214–15, 219, 228
Ecclesiologist (journal) 210, 212
ecumenical movement 231
Education Act (1944) 231
Edward VI 66, 69, 74, 75, 77, 78, 80
Elizabeth I 31, 66, *80*, 83, 87, 88–9, 90,
  91–2, 94, 95, 96, 99, 104, 108, 127,
  131
  Accession Day 116, 136
Elizabethan Settlement *see* Act of
  Uniformity (1559)
Ellman, Reverend Edward Boys 222–3
Ely, Cambridgeshire 138
English Heritage 233
English Hymnal, The 217
Erasmus, St 41
Erasmus, Desiderius: *Paraphrases on the
  New Testament* 76, 82, 98, 114
Essex 47, 109–10, 140, 163
Etheldreda, St 43–4
Eucharist, the 17, 35, 39, 48, 53, 67, 75,
  90, 129, 130, 131, 132, 133, 183, 185,
  216, 229
evangelicalism/evangelicals 194, 202,
  215, 217, 231
Evening Prayer 189, 190
Exeter, Devon 71–2, 194

Fairford, Gloucestershire: St Mary 63–5,
  64
Felix, St 43
Ferrar, Nicholas 156
Fifth Monarchists 155, 157
Five Mile Act (1665) 169
Flixton, Suffolk 127
Florence, Council of (1439) 39
Flower, Bernard 64
fonts 27, 28, 44–5, 46, 108, 109, 132, 151,
  158

Four Latin Doctors 44, 63
Foxe, John: *Actes and Monuments* 114, 118
Foxley, Norfolk: St Thomas *49*
France, war with 169, 194
fraternities 69–70
funeral services *see* burials/funerals
Furneaux, Hertfordshire 148

Garth, Reverend James 190
George, St 43
George III 183
Georgian Society 233
glebe land 25, 57, 175, 178, 207, 208
Gloucester (diocese) 72, 78
Gloucestershire 41, 63–5, *64*, 72, 77, 78, 93, *102*, 199–200, *201*
godparents 44, 45, 127
Goldsmith, Oliver 189
    The Vicar of Wakefield 189
Good Friday 32, 53, 70, 93, 117, 118
Gothic style 31, 46, 133, *135*, 145, 146, 167, 199, 210
Gough, Richard: *Observations concerning the Seates in Myddle...* 174
Great Alne, Warwickshire 218, 219
'Great Rebuilding' (1050–1150) 20, 22
Green Man, the 13
Gregorian chant 217
Gregory I, St ('the Great') 17, 23–4, 44, 63
Grindal, Edmund, Archbishop of York 114
guilds, religious 20, 38, 52, 69–70

Hailes, Gloucestershire: chancel *102*
Hampton Court Conference (1604) 126, 128
Hanbury family 180
Hardwick Church, Cambridgeshire 212
Hardy, Thomas: *Under the Greenwood Tree* 220
Harley, Sir Robert 145
Harrison, William: *Description of England* 109
Harvest Festival 220, 227
heating 28, 110
Heber, Reginald, bishop of Calcutta 217
Hell 39

Henry VIII 66, 89, 106
Herbert, George 134, 180, 207
    'The Church Floor' 134
    A Priest to the Temple 156
Hereford Cathedral 229
Herefordshire 27, 41, 87–8, *88*, 123–5, *124*, 140, 141, 145–6, *146*, 227–9
    see also Kilpeck
Heritage Lottery Fund 233
Herman, bishop of Ramsbury 20
Highnam, Gloucestershire: Holy Innocents 199–200, *201*
Hilton, Walter 38
    Ladder of Perfection 38
Hinton St Mary, Dorset: Roman villa 16
Historic Buildings Council 233
Holinshed, Ralph: *Chronicles* 104–5
Holy Communion *see* communion
Holy days 38, 52, 66, 67, 70, 71, 81, 118, 136
Holy Name, the 38
Holy Tables 73, 75, 83, 98, 101, 109, 114, 130–1, 132, 138, 146
holy water 44–5, 56, 69, 93, 117
holy-water clerks 57
Holy Week 18, 32, 52–3, 55
homilies, books of 71, 76, 98, 106–7, 108, 114
homosexuality 231
Hooker, Richard 75, 138
    Of the Laws of Ecclesiastical Polity 131
Hooper, John, Bishop of Gloucester 65, 72, 78
Hope, Alexander James Beresford 210
Host, the 26, 34, 35, 51, 52, 53, 55
    Elevation *see under* Mass(es)
houselling cloth 51
hymns 53, 91, 186–7, 194, 217
    The English Hymnal 217
    Hymns Ancient and Modern 217, 217, 222

images 23–4, 33, 41, 43–4, 65, 78, 133–4, 186, 211–2
    destruction of 67–9, 72–5, *73*, 81, 82, 92, *92*, 116, 151
    see also stained-glass windows; Virgin, images of the
incense 18, 33, 75, 131, 214, 216
Independents 149, 168

indulgences 36, 38–9
industrial revolution 178, 204

James I/James VI 126, 128
  Book of Sports 136
James II 169
Jenkins, Simon: *England's Thousand Best
  Churches* 9–10
Jerome, St 44, 63
Jewel, Bishop John 138
  Apologia 98
  Book of Homilies 106–7
John of Ford 25
Julian of Norwich 38
  The Sixteen Revelations of Divine Love
  38

Keble, John 203
  'Sermon on National Apostasy' 203
  The Christian Year 203
Kent 21, 25, 67, 69, 76, 173, 180, 189,
  207, 208, *209*, 210
Kilndown Church, Kent 210
Kilpeck, Herefordshire: St Mary and St
  David 13–14, *14*, *15*, 23
King's Norton, Leicestershire: St John
  the Baptist *188*
Kinwarton Church, Warwickshire 218–19

Lacock, Wiltshire 192
Lambeth, Council of (1281) 36
Lancashire 93, 149, 161
Langdale, Dr Alban 94
Larkin, Philip: 'Church Going' 7,
  235
Last Judgement, paintings of the 40
Last Supper, the 17, *53*, 75
Lateran Council (1215) 26, 36
Latin, use of 17, 28, 36, 67, 72, 77, 80,
  93, 105
Laud, William, Archbishop of
  Canterbury 125, 129, 131, 132, 134,
  147, 155, 167
Lay Folk's Mass Book 37–8
lecterns 27, 211
Leeds parish church 214
Leicestershire *113*, 146, *147*, 180, *188*
Leigh, Reverend Thomas, rector of
  Adlestrop 179–80
light wardens 58

lighting 28, 40, 58, 68, 74
Lilleshall, Suffolk 24
Lincolnshire 94, 155–6, 208–9
Lindisfarne: Celtic cross *16*
'lining-out' 191, 192
literacy and illiteracy 23–4, 36, 101, 111,
  137, 172–3
Little Birch, Herefordshire: St Mary 227
Little Gidding, Cambridgeshire 156
Little Shelford Church, Cambridgeshire
  212
Llanwarne, Herefordshire: Christ Church
  228–9
Local Government Act (1894) 205
Lollards 36–7, 38
London: All Saints, Margaret Street 200,
  218
London, Council of (1129) 58
Long Melford, Suffolk
  Holy Trinity 31–5, *32*, 36, 55, 59
  rectory 207
Long Parliament 147–8
Longstanton Church, Cambridgeshire 212
Lord's Prayer/Paternoster 28, 50, 67, 80,
  98, 107, 116, 185, 189
Lower Peover, Cheshire: St Oswald
  68
Ludham, Norfolk: St Catherine 78, *79*, *81*
Luther, Martin 66
Lyons, Council of (1274) 39

MacCulloch, Diarmaid 119
Mace, Thomas: *Musick's Monument* 191–2
Marbecke, John: *Booke of common praier
  noted* 105
Marbury, Essex 163
March, Cambridgeshire: St Wendreda *42*
marriage 23, 26, 47, 55, 68, 114, 157,
  159–60, 148, 207, 220
Marriage Act (1753) 190
Marriage and Registration Act (1653)
  160
Martyn, Roger 31–3, *53*, 59
martyrs 25, 78, *117*, 118
Mary I/Marian revival 77–8, 83, 88, 92,
  97, 98, 99, 118
Mary II 170
Maskell, William
  *The Ancient Liturgy of the Church of
  England* 214

*Monumenta Ritualia Ecclesiae
Anglicanae* 214
Mass(es) 17–18, 20, 27, 28, 44, 48, 50,
53, 56, *56*, 216
bread and wine 17, 18, 26, 48
Elevation of the Host 18, 36, *37*, 48,
50, 71, 89
and liturgical books 36, 37, *37*
post-Reformation 69, 71, 77, 89, 101
requiem 40, *56*, 70, 74, 82, 160–1
see also communion
matins 103, *187*, 189
Maundy Thursday 53, 117, 218
Methodists 186–7, 194, 202, 207, 217
Michael, St 44
Michaelmas 189
Mildenhall, Wiltshire: St John the Baptist
167–8, *168*, 199
minsters 19–20
Mirk, John 24
missionaries 16–17
monastic houses/monks 20, 26, 66, 93,
123–5, *124*
Montagu, Bishop Richard 139
Morebath, Devon 80, 82–3, 97–9
Morning Prayer 189, 216, 217, 218
Morris (William) & Co 211
Morritt, Thomas 78
Much Birch, Herefordshire: St Mary and
St Thomas à Becket 227–8
Muggletonians 157
music and singing 40, 53, 55, 70, 91,
105–6, 114, 191–4, *193*, 214–15,
217–18, 220
see also hymns; psalms
musicians' galleries *133*, 167, 192
Myddle Church, Shropshire 174, *176–7*
mystery plays 234
mystics 38, 156

Neale, Dr John Mason 210
Neile, Richard, Archbishop of York 137
*New and Easie method to learn to sing by
book, A* 192
Newman, Cardinal John Henry 203, 222
Nicaea, Second Council of (787) 24
Nonconformists 169
Norfolk *33*, 38, 43–4, *49*, 73, 78, 79, *80*,
107, 138, 175, 178, 182–3, 217, 219
Norman style 13, 210

Northamptonshire 134, 140
Northumbria 22, 103
Norwich, Norfolk 138, 219
Nottinghamshire 132, 138
Nowell, Alexander, Dean of St Paul's 107

Olney Hymns 194
organs 105–6, 151, 192, 214–15, 217,
218, 220, 222, 229
Osmund, bishop of Salisbury 18
Oxford Movement/Tractarians 75, 186,
200, 203–4, 210, 213–14, 214, 217,
218, 222, 229
Tracts for the Times 203
Oxfordshire 26, 44, *45*, *133*, 207, 208

Palm Sunday 18, 34, 35, 52–3, 70, 103,
117, 189
'papists' 93
pardons 38–9, 66
Parish and People movement 229
parish chests *68*, 69, 75, 88, 114
parish clerks 114
parish officers 114
parish register 68–9, 80, 88, 114
parish vestry 205, *205*
parishes, 'open' and 'closed' 206
Parker, Matthew, Archbishop of
Canterbury 129
Advertisements (1566) 108
Parkyn, Robert 70
Parochial Libraries Act (1709) 173
Parry, Thomas Gambier 200
parsonages, nineteenth-century 206–7
parsons 180, *181*, 182–3
Partrishow, Herefordshire: St Issui 87–8, *88*
Passenham, Northamptonshire 134
patens *25*, 27
Paternoster *see* Lord's Prayer
Patrington, Humberside: St Patrick *54*, *55*
paxes 33, 50, *51*, 77, 117
penances 39, 50–1, 67, 111, 140, 191
Pentecost *see* Whitsun
Perpendicular style 31, 41
Peterborough, Cambridgeshire *133*, 134,
138
Pevsner, Nikolaus 8, 9, 228
The Buildings of England 8
pews 40–1, 109, 110, 112, 132, 137, 174,
176–7, 187–9, 209, 210, 213

pilgrimages 36, 65, 66, 67, 68
Pilkington, Reverend J. G.: *The Spiritual Garland* 217
Piper, John 9
piscinas 26
Pius V, Pope 95
plate, silver 133, 151, 185
Pluralities Act (1838) 206
poor relief 58, 98, 205
porches 23, 43, 45, 46–7, 47, 65
porticus 21–2
Prayer Books *see* Book of Common Prayer
preaching *see* sermons
Presbyterians 145, 149, 168, 169
Prideaux, John 131
primers 36, 37, 72
processions 69, 98
    see also Rogationtide
Protestants/Protestantism 77, 95, 118–19
    see also Church of England; Methodists; Presbyterians; Puritans
psalms 104, 106, 117, 160, 189, 191, 194, 217
Pugin, A. W. N. 210
pulpits 44, 56, 75, 87, 108, 109, 114, 132, 137
    three-decker 186, 210, 213
Purchas, John 214
    Directorium Anglicanum 214
purgatory 39, 66, 74
Puritans 95, 96–7, 101, 108, 111, 125–7, 129, 130, 135, 145, 147–9,151–3, 155, 158, 234
    and communion 189–90
    see also Sabbatarianism
Pusey, Edward Bouverie 203
pyxes 26, 33, 40, 53, 55, 70, 83, 116

Quakers 157, 170, 179, 191
Queen Anne's Bounty 175

Radwinter, Essex: St Mary 47, 140
Ranters 157
Ranworth, Norfolk: St Helen 33, 43–4
rebellion, sixteenth-century 71–2, 83
rectories, nineteenth-century 206–7
rectors 26, 57–8
recusants 31, 36, 96, 103–4, 157
Reformation, the 65–8, 70–8, 81–3, 129

iconoclasm 23, 24, 31, 40, 43, 64–5, 68, 69, 74–5, 74, 107, 116, 200, 223
relics/reliquaries 24–5, 33, 52, 53, 65, 67, 68
Remembrance Sunday 227
Reproaches, the 53
Requiem Masses 56, 70, 74, 82, 160–1
reredos 167, 185, 199
Restoration, the 169, 170–1, 174, 185, 191
Richard, St 41
Ringland, Norfolk: St Peter 73
Roberts, Reverend Arthur 217
Rochester, Kent 207, 208
Rogationtide 52, 70, 91, 118, 127
Rolle, Richard 38
Roman Britain 14, 16
Romanesque style 13, 22–3
Roods 23–4, 32, 40, 53, 77, 83, 108
    painted 78, 79
rood-lofts 34, 76, 92, 93, 98
rood-screens 32, 33, 43, 48, 51
rosaries 67, 72, 93
Rottingdean, Sussex: St Margaret (stained glass window) 211
royal arms 81, 87, 108, 116, 171, 185
Rycote, Oxfordshire: St Michael 133

Sabbatarianism 97, 126, 136, 153, 154
Sacrament, the 74, 78, 83
    see also Host, the
sacraments *see* Seven Sacraments
St Helen, Lancashire 93
saints 43–4, 49, 65, 66, 67, 118, 216, 223
saints' days 52, 71, 136
Sanderson, Robert 155–6
Sarum rite 18–19
screens 26, 108, 151, 228
    see also reredos; rood-screens
Scudamore, John, Viscount 125, 141
sculptural decoration 13, 14, 15, 23, 27, 199
    destruction of 116, 150
seating
    for clergy 26–7
    for congregation 28, *see* pews
Sebastian, St 41
Secker, Thomas, Archbishop of Canterbury 190

Separatists 157
sermons 56, 70–1, 75, 96, 102, 103, 105,
   106, 110–11, 117, 126, 137–8, 180,
   189, 216–17
Seven Deadly Sins 36, 51, 56
Seven Sacraments 36, 44, 56
   see also baptism; communion; confirma-
   tion; Eucharist; marriage; penance
Seven Virtues 36, 56
Seven Works of Mercy 36, 51, 56
Seymour, Lady Jane 66
Seymour, Reverend Richard 218–19
Shaxton, Nicholas, bishop of Salisbury 69
Sherburn, Yorkshire 78
Shere, Surrey 180
Sherlock, Thomas, bishop of Salisbury
   194
Shirley, Sir Robert 145–6
singing *see* music and singing
'singing cakes' 53
Six Articles (1539) 69
Smarden Church, Kent 76
Society for Promoting Christian
   Knowledge (SPCK) 172–3, 192
Society for the Protection of Ancient
   Buildings 232–3
Solemn League and Covenant 145
South Lindsey, Lincolnshire: restoration
   of churches 208–9
South Cerney, Gloucestershire: All
   Hallows 77
Spain, war with/Spanish Armada 89, 99,
   118, 169
SPCK *see* Society for Promoting Christian
   Knowledge
Spectator 173
'squarsons' 179
stained glass windows 24, 63–4, 124, 199,
   211, *211*
Stalmine, Lancashire 93
Stanton Harcourt, Oxfordshire: screen 26
Staunton Harold, Leicestershire: Holy
   Trinity 146, *147*
Sternhold, Thomas, and Hopkins, John:
   The whole booke of psalms 106, 192
Storgursey, Somerset 110–11
Stowe, Buckinghamshire 110
Street, G. E. 208
Stubbes, Philip: *Anatomy of Abuses*
   111–12

Suffolk 24, 40, *115*, 127, 151
   see also Long Melford
Sunday schools 220
superstition, popular 55–6, 220, 223
surplices 75, 89, 91, 114, 126, 138, 140,
   148
   choristers' 214, 216
Sussex 94, 208, *211*, 217–18, 222
Swing riots (1830–32) 208
Synod of Whitby (664) 17, 18

Tallis, Thomas 217
Tame, Sir Edmund 64–5
Tame, John 63, 64
Temple family 110
Ten Articles (1536) 67
Ten Commandments/Decalogue 36, 56,
   67, 72, 80, 87, 98, 107, 108, 116, 185
Test Act (1673) 169
Test and Corporation Act (1828) 202
Theodore of Tarsus 18
Thirty-Nine Articles (1563) 98
Tithe Acts (1696) 178–9
tithes 25, 57–8, 112, 162, 175, *178*,
   178–9, 207
Toleration Act (1689) 170, 171, 175
tombs 22, 40–41, 58–9, 112, *113*
towers 22, *22*, 65
Tractarians *see* Oxford Movement
Traherne, Thomas 156
training colleges 208
transept 22
Transfiguration of Christ 52
transubstantiation 26, 36, 69, 89
Trental of St Gregory 56
Trigge, Reverend Francis 94
triptychs 31–2
Trychay, Sir Christopher 80, 83, 98
Tudor style 47
tympana 13, 23

Upton-by-Southwell Church,
   Nottinghamshire 132

Vaughan, Henry 156
vestments 16, 26, 27–8, 33–4, 73, 90, 92,
   89, 90–1, 93, 97, 98, 101, 151, 211,
   214, 216
   see also surplices
vestries 22, 26

vicarages, nineteenth-century 206–7
vicars 26, 57, 58
Victorian era 31, 185–6, 206–9, 210–20, 222–3, 228
Victorian Society 233
Virgin, images of the 24, 33, 34, 43, *43*, 65, 151
visitations 27–8, 77, 92, 139, 151, 175
Vitalian, Pope 18

Wake, William, Archbishop of Canterbury: *Exposition of the Doctrine of the Church of England* 186
Warde family 180
water, holy *see* holy water
Watts, Isaac 194
Webb, Benjamin 210
weddings *see* marriage
Welborn, Lincolnshire 94
Wells, Somerset
  St Cuthbert *150*
  training college 208
Wells, Reverend John 151
Wenhaston, Suffolk: St Peter 40
Wesley, Charles 194
Wesley, John 186, 187
Westhall, Suffolk: St Andrew *115*
Weston Longueville, Norfolk 182–3
Wheatly, Charles: *The Church of*

England's Man's Companion, or, A Rational Illustration of . . . the Book of Common Prayer 183, *184*, 185
White, Sir Thomas 180
Whitsun (Pentecost) 52, 71, 189, 222
Wilberforce, William 202
William III 169–70
Wiltshire *19*, 23, 149, 175, 190, 192, 207
  see also Mildenhall
Winchester, Hampshire 178
Wing, Berkshire 110
women 58, 83, 109–10, 231
  see also churching
Woodforde, Parson James: diaries 182–3, 192–3
Woodrising, Norfolk 217
Woodyer, Henry 200
wool trade 36, 63
Wormelow Hundred 227
Wulfric, St 25
Wycliffe, John 36

Yalding, Kent 180
York
  Archbishops *see* Grindal, Edmund; Neile, Richard
  Consistory Court 194
Yorkshire 70, 78, 215